GLORIA REPP

THE STORY OF ISOBEL KUHN

JOURNEYFORTH

Greenville, South Carolina

Library of Congress Cataloging-in-Publication Data

Repp, Gloria, 1941—
    Nothing daunted : the story of Isobel Kuhn / by Gloria Repp.
        p.   cm.
    ISBN 0-89084-753-3
    1. Kuhn, Isobel—Juvenile literature.   2. Missionaries—China—
    Biographies—Juvenile literature.   3. Missionaries—United States—
    Biographies—Juvenile literature.   4. China Inland Mission. [1. Kuhn,
    Isobel.   2. Missionaries.   3. Women—Biography.   4. China Inland
    Mission.]   I. Title.
    BV3427.K8R47   1994
    266'.0092—dc20
    [B]
                                                                    94-15531
                                                                        CIP
                                                                         AC

Nothing Daunted: The Story of Isobel Kuhn

Edited by Manda Cooper
Cover Illustration by Roger Bruckner
Cover design by Nathan Hutcheon

© 1994 by BJU Press
Greenville, SC 29614
JourneyForth Books is a division of BJU Press

Printed in the United States of America

ISBN 978-0-89084-753-4

15   14   13   12   11   10   9   8   7   6   5

For Russ
my husband, my friend

Acknowledgement

Excerpts from Isobel Kuhn's books and letters
by kind permission of OMF (IHQ) Ltd.

Sources:
Ascent to the Tribes
By Searching
In the Arena
Nests Above the Abyss
Precious Things of the Lasting Hills
Second Mile People
Stones of Fire

Contents

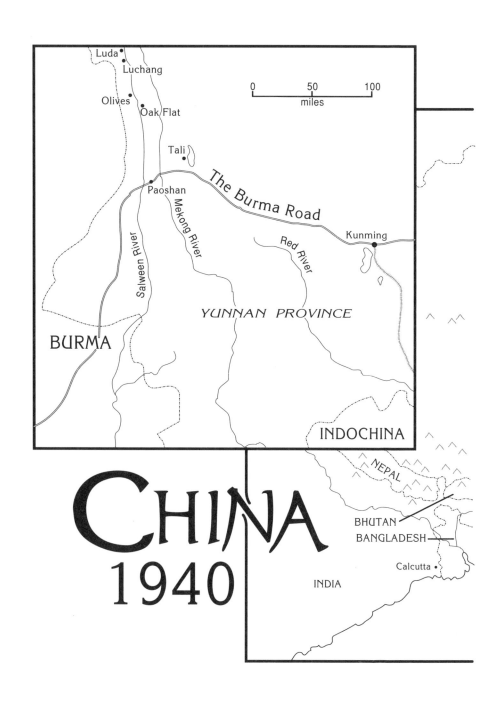

Luda
Luchang
Olives
Oak/Flat

0   50   100
miles

Tali

Paoshan   The Burma Road

Salween River

Mekong River

Red River

Kunming

YUNNAN PROVINCE

BURMA

INDOCHINA

NEPAL

CHINA
1940

BHUTAN
BANGLADESH

Calcutta

INDIA

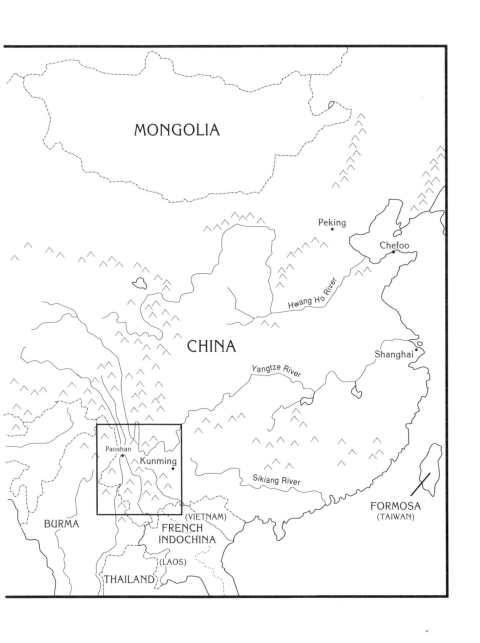

MONGOLIA

Peking

Chefoo

Hwang Ho River

CHINA

Yangtze River

Shanghai

Paoshan

Kunming

Sikiang River

BURMA

(VIETNAM)

FRENCH
INDOCHINA

FORMOSA
(TAIWAN)

(LAOS)

THAILAND

Prologue: The Valley

1921

Vancouver, British Columbia

Isobel clicked the front door shut and bent to take off her shoes. The silence of the dark house pressed against her. She brushed past the hat rack that stood near the door, then she frowned. It could have been a good party tonight, but everything was different now, without Ben.

She went up the stairway through the shadows. Daddy wasn't home—that was a relief; perhaps Mother had gone to bed and no one would ask her anything. But a light from her mother's bedroom shone into the hall, and as Isobel passed, a soft voice called, "Well, how did it go? Was Ben there?"

Isobel paused in the doorway. "It was fine, Mother. They had a saxophone in the band, and we tried a new version of the fox trot. But my feet are about to give out—I've got to go to bed."

"Oh, yes, it's past midnight." Her mother's voice sharpened with anxiety. "I was hoping you would come to church with us in the morning."

A weight far heavier than physical exhaustion clamped down upon Isobel. "I don't think so." She turned down the hall.

Wearily she went through her careful bedtime ritual, fluffing up her pillow and making sure that the sheets and blankets were smooth. Perhaps tonight the tears would not come; perhaps she would be able to sleep.

As soon as she closed her eyes, she saw Ben's rugged face; he was still sneering. She snatched at the sheet and pulled it taut.

He'd been all she could ever wish for—a born leader, a star athlete, a wonderful dancer—and for the past two years she had given him her heart's devotion. Ben came from a good family, so Mother approved, even when they became secretly engaged.

Everything had changed the day she found out that he was dating Reba behind her back. And all Ben could say was, "You don't suppose, do you, that after we are married, I'm not going to take other women out sometimes?"

Isobel jerked herself upright and rearranged her pillow. Forget Ben. Think about something else. That dress she'd worn tonight— she was getting tired of it. Maybe change the ribbons? How about narrow ones, moss green? Silk? Or perhaps that new fabric called rayon. And hemlines were going up, so she'd shorten the skirt too, no matter what Mother said. Maybe that would help. Isobel sighed. She'd felt so wilted tonight. Perhaps it wasn't the dress.

Today in class, Dr. Sedgewick had discussed a line from one of Thomas Hardy's poems: "the gloomy aisles of this wailful world." I know all about that gloomy, hopeless feeling, she thought. But at least I'm learning to think things through for myself, like Hardy.

She smiled wryly in the darkness. Good old Dr. Sedgewick. Three years ago during his freshman literature class, she'd learned that no thinking person believed in the Bible anymore. She'd tried to explain the modern approach to her parents. "Dr. Sedgewick says that you can't take the Genesis account literally, and scholars have serious questions about other parts of the Bible too."

Daddy frowned, so she'd hurried on. "We're studying some wonderful poets—Matthew Arnold and Thomas Hardy. Hardy says that a God who is both great and good couldn't exist, and the more I think about it, the more I wonder if he might be right. There's really no scientific proof for God, you know."

Mother was upset, of course, and Daddy had started praying for her all the more. But her new philosophy had its benefits. She could be part of the intellectual crowd at the university and join in their discussions on the Absolute. She didn't have to waste time on Bible reading and prayer. And Sunday mornings were a good time to catch up on sleep after a late night of dancing.

Isobel yawned, then waited to see if she felt any sleepier. She just couldn't be tired tomorrow. She had that paper to type, research on Dante's poetry to finish, and another two hundred pages to read. In spite of so many accomplishments in her English honors course, she couldn't be sure that her next grades would be as high. And they *had* to be.

She stared at the dark rectangle of her window, closed her eyes, then opened them again as the post office clock struck three. Maybe she should get up and memorize her lines for the new play next week? No, if she didn't get some rest, she'd be ill again tomorrow. The bitter tears welled up.

Sleep finally came, too late to be refreshing, and once again Isobel had to drag herself out of bed in the morning. Determined to make a success of her senior year, she battled her sleeplessness each night and rushed through the whirl of university life each day. Besides her studies, she had play practices for the upcoming tour by the university's Players Club, and in the evenings she could count on being asked to one dance or another.

Everybody on campus knew who Isobel Miller was—a slender, dark-haired girl with sparkling brown eyes, a member of the Student Council, a gifted comedy actress who had won lifetime membership in the Players Club. And how she could dance! The *Varsity* yearbook for 1922 defined her with a caption next to her picture: ". . . oh, the tilt of her heels when she dances!"

If only Mother weren't always harping at her about going to church. She was the one who'd wanted Isobel to move in the best social circles—that was why she'd insisted on speech and dance lessons. Couldn't she see that a girl with old-fashioned religious beliefs just didn't belong?

Daddy didn't say nearly as much as Mother, but Isobel knew he was grieved. Late one night he had come in and knelt by her bed. When she had been small, his voice there beside her had comforted and warmed her. Now, listening to him pray only made her angry. As he rose from his knees, she said, "I know you mean it well, but praying doesn't go beyond the ceiling, you know." He didn't argue, although she almost wished he would. He turned away with a groan, and she remembered the sound of his heartbreak through many long nights to come.

Isobel's sleepless nights lengthened into weeks, draining her already-slim reserves. By the time December came, with its dreary fog and rain, she began to wonder how tired she'd have to get before she could really sleep. The weeks dragged on toward Christmas.

I've got to stop thinking about Ben, she told herself on yet another sleepless rainy night. She had been so sure that he'd make her happy for always, and the girls were still saying that she'd been a fool to send him away. You couldn't expect a man like Ben to stay faithful— "not in these modern days," the girls had said.

A dismal pattering of rain against the window filled her room, and Isobel twisted a corner of the sheet into a knot. Maybe her standards were too high. Maybe she had been foolish to let Ben go. No, she replied for the hundredth time. I don't want that kind of life. I want—

What is there to want? she thought, suddenly desperate. What is it I want? She tried to calm herself by thinking about what she did have. Good grades. And looks. But it was all so much work— and for what? Weariness overwhelmed her, but not sleep.

She tried to shut out the sound of the incessant rain and reached for her new volume of Hardy's poems. He would have something to say. She turned the pages. "In Death Divided," "Rain on a Grave," "Over the Coffin." Not those. Here, what about this one: "To Life."

> O Life with the sad seared face
>   I weary of seeing thee,
> And thy draggled cloak, and thy hobbling pace,
>   And thy too-forced pleasantry!

Tears blurred the rest, and she pushed the book aside. Hardy was right. Life meant only suffering; it wasn't worth the struggle. She pulled herself to her feet and stood hunched beside the bed. The darkness seemed to whirl around her, and she could think only one thought: there's a bottle in the bathroom cabinet marked *Poison.* . . .

Her feet started toward the hall. She paused, her fingers tightening on the doorknob. What was that? Daddy, groaning in his sleep. She drew a ragged breath. He would be the one to find her. Suddenly she saw how it would be: he would think she'd gone to hell. Her hand slipped from the doorknob. Even at the bottom of despair she could not be cruel.

She stumbled back to bed and crouched there, hating herself and her dilemma. In the dark emptiness, a line from Dante's poem came unbidden to her mind. *In His will is our peace.*

In *His* will? Slowly she raised herself. Dante the thinker, the poet of poets, believed in God. God's will was important to him.

She lifted her face to the darkness. "God, if there be a God," she said, "if You will prove to me that You are, and if You will give me peace, I will give You my whole life."

She shivered, conscious now of the winter night. She slid under the rumpled blankets and pulled them up to her chin. She slept.

Ye shall seek me, and find me,
when ye shall search for me with all your heart.
Jeremiah 29:13

Part I: The Foothills

1922-33

Chapter One

A sparkle of water through the trees caught Isobel's eye. Was it the lake? She glanced at the man who had picked her up at the dock, and he nodded. "We're almost there."

She leaned out the car window, trying to peer around each bend in the road as they swept through a thick stand of pines and firs. Last July she'd had misgivings about coming to The Firs for a Bible conference, but that was before she knew Mrs. Whipple.

As hostess of The Firs, Mrs. Whipple had not only invited Isobel to come, she had paid the boat ticket from Vancouver to Bellingham, Washington. I wonder what she's doing right now, Isobel thought. Probably rushing around, getting ready for the conference. Is she looking forward to seeing me again? I know she's been praying for me all these months.

She stared into the trees. Two years ago, she thought, I wasn't even sure that God existed. And look how much He's done for me!

After that December night when He had answered her cry for peace, she'd decided to search for Him in the Bible. Not the Old Testament, she'd thought, remembering the questions her professors had raised. She'd try the Gospels—they were an authentic historical record.

For several months she had studied the Bible on her own; she had prayed—cautiously—and God had answered her prayers, even the selfish ones. Prayer must be more than a form of psychological release, she had concluded, no matter what anyone said. That spring Mother had started attending an evening Bible class at the Vancouver Bible Institute and had begged her to come too. She'd gone, unwillingly at first, and then with an increasing hunger to know Jesus Christ.

Before long, it was summer and she'd made her first visit to The Firs, where she had met Mrs. Whipple. After that she had spent a lonely year teaching school while she lived in a boarding house in Vancouver. She'd read the Bible from cover to cover, learning to depend on it for her spiritual growth and encouragement. As God spoke to her through His Word, she'd turned away from dancing and the other amusements of her old life. Nothing could compare to the delight of fellowship with Him.

Many nights she had pondered Mrs. Whipple's quiet remark: "Isobel, I've always found God's will through His Word, this Book." That was exactly what she wanted—to discover His will and to serve Him with all her heart.

Isobel stirred from her reverie and sighed. Yes, God had been good to her. Even so, she still wasn't sure what He wanted her to do with her life.

The car swung around one last curve, then they were pulling into a parking space ringed by tall fir trees. Mrs. Whipple was hurrying down the path, her round face shining with welcome. Isobel scrambled out of the car and ran to hug her.

"Well now, Isobel Miller," she exclaimed, her laugh rippling just the way Isobel remembered. "If you haven't grown as skinny as a stick!"

Isobel smiled. "I have a lot to tell you."

"I'm looking forward to that." Mrs. Whipple's bright eyes were lingering on Isobel's face. "I've enjoyed your letters, but there's nothing like having a good talk. Maybe tonight?"

"Tonight for sure! I know you have to get back to work—I'll never understand how you keep everything running so smoothly around here."

"Where do these go?" The man stood beside them with her suitcases.

"Oh, thank you," Isobel said. "Just put them up on the porch and I'll get them later. I've got to take a quick look around."

A few minutes later Mrs. Whipple returned to her work and Isobel hurried down a trail that wound through the trees. Here was the tiny cabin she had lived in last summer, and the sunlit clearing where they'd met for Bible study. And this was the big old Firs cabin where campers had shared testimonies in front of a crackling fire. She darted inside, smiling to herself, and was almost to the fireplace before she realized that a dark-haired man sat there.

"Oh, excuse me," she exclaimed, and she scurried out, wondering briefly who he was.

That night she was surprised to see the same man sitting on the platform. When the meeting began, the chairman introduced him as the conference speaker: Mr. J. O. Fraser, a missionary with the China Inland Mission.

As he came to the pulpit, Isobel studied the tall, rugged-looking man with new interest. She had met several workers from the CIM, since her parents often invited missionaries to stay in their home. And this winter she'd read the life story of Hudson Taylor, *The Growth of a Soul.* His experiences of proving God had challenged her to trust God more deeply, and she had been drawn to the mission he had founded, the China Inland Mission. She had even wondered whether the Lord might want her to be a missionary in China.

She leaned forward as J. O. Fraser began to speak. One day while he was preaching in a Chinese marketplace he had noticed some dark-faced men who wore turbans. Their clothes, trimmed with shells and silver ornaments, were different from anything he had seen. After watching them for a while, he had tried speaking to them in trade-language Chinese. He learned that they had no written language and that they came from the Lisu tribe, high in the mountains beside the Salween River.

When Mr. Fraser described his trips back into Lisu country, Isobel felt as if she were climbing the narrow path right behind him. Towering mountains rose on all sides, and far below, the Salween River thundered its way through a rocky canyon. What was this, just ahead? Five weather-beaten bamboo shacks clinging to the mountainside. A Lisu village! Dogs rushed out, barking, and people poured from the huts with welcoming shouts. "*Ma-pa* (the man teacher) is here!"

Mr. Fraser began to explain what life was like in those Lisu villages, and when he sat down at the end of an hour, Isobel glanced at her watch in surprise. How could the meeting be over so soon?

Each day that week she looked forward to the evening service. One night Mr. Fraser told how he had learned to speak Lisu as he sat by their smoky fires, listening and asking questions. After several years he had transcribed an alphabet and a written language—now called the Fraser script—so they could learn to read the Bible for themselves.

Another evening he described the Lisu people themselves: their warm, generous hearts; their love of music; their lives as farmers on the rocky hillsides. Then his eyes darkened. He told how every part of Lisu life was affected by the fear of demons. When a child fell sick or a pig ran away, they took it to mean that the demons were angry, and they hurried to offer a sacrifice. Satan's hold over these people was very strong, Mr. Fraser said, and he'd found that prayer was the best weapon he had against such a powerful enemy.

Night after night before she fell asleep, Isobel thought about Mr. Fraser's messages. She had listened to missionary stories ever since she was a child, but this was different. It seemed that the Lisu people and their needs had reached out and grabbed a piece of her heart.

At the last meeting of the conference, Mr. Fraser told the audience that he was looking for volunteers to help him reach the Lisu tribe. But, he warned, it would take hard work and sacrifice; he needed consecrated young men.

Isobel sat still, gripping the Bible in her lap. Lord, she prayed, I'd be willing to go. Only I'm not a man.

Chapter Two

Home again two days later, Isobel eyed her mother warily when her father mentioned that he had invited Mr. Fraser for a week's visit. Right from the first, Mother had objected to Isobel's idea of becoming a missionary; what would happen when this missionary from the China Inland Mission arrived at their home?

Isobel braced herself for the worst, but when Mother found out that their guest was a graduate of London University and an accomplished musician, her frosty manner thawed visibly. At mealtimes they enjoyed interesting conversations, and in the evenings they listened to Mr. Fraser's brilliant performances on the piano.

No matter how charming Mr. Fraser might be, Isobel knew that her mother would not change her mind. Mother was hoping she would settle down with someone like the nice Christian boy who had been so attentive this summer. Or get involved in some kind of ocal Christian work. But to go off and evangelize a heathen country like China? "How will you live? You'll be an object of charity," Mother had said. "And people will think it's because you can't find anyone to marry. What a disgrace!"

"No, you know that's not it!" Isobel had cried. "You're the president of the Women's Missionary Society, and you know that those people in China have never heard about Christ. They don't have a single Bible for a whole village, and look—we've got a dozen in this house alone.''

But Mother resisted, and Murray, her older brother, kept trying to convince Isobel that she should make more of her life. Their discussions always seemed to end with Mother storming out of the room or bursting into tears. One day her mother exclaimed, ''If you go to China, it will be over my dead body. I will never consent.''

Isobel had fled to her bedroom, sobbing. ''Lord, what am I going to do?'' she whispered. ''I want to obey You, but I know I should honor my parents. Please, help me!''

She brushed at her tears and tried to think it through. God must have a way for her to solve this problem. Perhaps Mr. Fraser—that was it! Maybe he would give her some good advice while he was here.

As the missionary's visit drew to a close, she looked for an opportunity to talk to him in private. One day Mother asked her to show him the beach, and Isobel quickly agreed. As they walked along the sand, she poured out her desire to go to China—perhaps to the Lisu tribe—as a missionary.

Mr. Fraser gazed at the ocean waves, his blue grey eyes thoughtful. ''Missionary life can be lonely,'' he said. Then he told Isobel about some of his own experiences. She listened gravely, realizing that he was trying to warn her about the personal sacrifices she might have to make.

After he finished, she told him about her mother's determination to keep her at home, and he heard her out in silence. When it seemed that he wasn't going to say anything more, she ventured to ask if he would underline a verse in her Bible to take along when she went to Bible school—if the Lord opened the way. He turned to I Peter, chapter 5. *Casting all your care upon him; for he careth for you. Be sober, be vigilant; because your adversary the devil, as a roaring lion, walketh about, seeking whom he may devour. Whom resist—* He underlined the last words twice, then stared out across the ocean.

Finally he said, ''Miss Miller, I have sensed that Satan is opposing you and working through your mother and your brother.

We are taught 'whom resist' when it comes to obstacles produced by the Devil. I think that this should be your stand. I have a prayer that I often use when I run into problems: *If this obstacle be from Thee, Lord, I accept it; but if it be from Satan, I refuse him and all his works in the name of Calvary."*

I want to remember every word of this, Isobel thought, and she memorized his prayer.

Then Mr. Fraser added soberly, "I wonder if you will ever get to China. You are young, and you have great obstacles to face...." He paused and seemed to lose himself in contemplation.

Isobel waited in silence. Finally he went on. He warned her that even when she got to Bible school, Satan might try to lure her away. For instance, she might receive a telegram saying that her mother was sick. Instead of rushing home, Mr. Fraser suggested that she ask a Christian friend to check on the details while she started packing. Then she could decide what to do.

As they strolled back from the beach, questions whirled through Isobel's mind. She already knew that sacrifices would be part of missionary life, and today Mr. Fraser had spoken plainly about his own sufferings. Had she thought up this whole idea of being a missionary because she was tired of teaching school? Did she dare to face Satan's opposition? Was she sure this was something God wanted her to do?

Her gaze lingered on the broad expanse of the ocean, and suddenly her fears seemed as inconsequential as the gulls that wheeled and cried overhead. Yes. God had clearly led her this far, and He had brought Mr. Fraser into her life for a reason. Her hand tightened around the Bible she carried. She had Mr. Fraser's verse—her verse now—and the Lord Himself would make her strong enough to *resist.*

In the days that followed J. O. Fraser's visit, Isobel felt more certain than ever that China was God's place for her, and she wanted to get on with His plan. She had graduated from the University of British Columbia in 1922, two years ago already, but the China

Inland Mission required her to get some Bible training. And before she could do that, she had two problems to solve: Mother, and money.

She had no savings to draw upon; any money left from her teacher's salary had gone to pay off college debts. And her parents didn't have any money to help her with, she knew that. In fact, Daddy had warned her right from the start that he would give her nothing. "I'm willing for you to be a missionary," he said. "But I won't help you financially. You might just as well learn to trust God for your finances now. If God wants you to go, He will provide the funds apart from me."

His words surprised her at first, but she decided to take them as God's way of telling her to trust Him more completely. Like Hudson Taylor. Long before he ever went to China, the famous missionary had taught himself to depend on God for everything. I'm not going to be discouraged, Isobel thought; God knows what I need. Then she smiled. Hadn't He already done something remarkable through her friend Marjorie Harrison?

Marjorie, too, had dreamed of going to China. For years she had saved every penny toward the cost of her equipment, but just recently she had been turned down by the Mission Council because of her frail health. When Isobel heard of it, she had protested indignantly. "Just because you have bad headaches—"

"No, listen, Isobel, the Lord doesn't make any mistakes," Marjorie had said. "And you know what I asked Him to do?"

Isobel shook her head, silenced by her friend's calm words.

"I asked Him to show me someone I could send to China in my place. And it's you!"

"Oh, Marjorie, I couldn't take your money—"

"But haven't you been praying for the money to go to Bible school?"

"Well, yes, but—"

"Then it's settled." Marjorie had given her a triumphant smile. "I'm sure this is what the Lord wants me to do. I'd like for you to go to Moody Bible Institute—that's where I went. It's a two-year program. I don't have enough money for your whole two years, but I can pay your train fare to Chicago and your room and board for the first year." She frowned. "I wish I had more to give you. You'll need other things, like bus fare and warm clothes—"

Isobel threw her arms around her friend. "Oh, Marjorie, don't worry!" How could she fret about clothes when the Lord had so wonderfully helped her with this first step? "My biggest obstacle right now is my mother. She might not agree to let me go, and the Bible says to honor our parents." For a while longer, Isobel and Marjorie had talked, then they had prayed together, and that night, Isobel had gone home rejoicing.

Marjorie's gift was an encouragement, but nothing happened for weeks afterward. The middle of summer passed, and Isobel began to wonder if she was making a mistake. Should she teach school for another year and think it over? One Friday near the end of July 1924, she sat alone in the kitchen and tried to sort out her difficulties.

Really, it still looks impossible, she thought. First, Mother has to decide to let me go—that will take a miracle. Then I have to notify the school board at least a month ahead of time. Then I have to apply to Moody. And—the money! I've got to find out whether Moody lets students work while they're going to school.

She put her head in her hands. "Lord, what shall I do? If something doesn't happen this weekend, I'll have to teach school in the fall."

Then she remembered the person Mother had been hoping she would marry. He was a pleasant enough Christian with a good education and a fine family, but when he'd proposed to her this summer, Isobel could not give him a definite answer. She'd just found out that he too was applying to Moody. Would that change Mother's mind?

She lifted her head and absent-mindedly traced a scratch across the top of the kitchen table. Did she dare to mention Moody one more time? Mother had become so hysterical about the whole subject of China and Bible training that Daddy had warned her not to talk about it. But Mother would be interested in the plans of this particular young man.

When her mother walked in and began taking dishes from the kitchen cupboard, Isobel mentioned the boy she'd been thinking about. "I've just heard that he is applying to Moody for this fall. Really, Mother, I don't know why you are so against my going."

Her mother paused. "He is a fine young man." She put a plate down on the counter. "And who said I was against your going? You can go if you like; you'll have to pay your own expenses, that is all."

"Really?" Isobel wanted to jump up and cheer. "Do you really mean it? Then I'll write and resign from my teaching job."

"Yes." Mother sounded amazingly calm. "You may go to Moody if you are so set on it. But I didn't say you could go to China."

A song of praise bubbled up inside her. Oh, thank you, Lord. Thank you! Now she could write that letter to the school board; she could apply to Moody. Her thoughts raced on to the next problem. What about work? Before she could apply to Moody, she *had* to find out about working, and there was no time left to write to the school. If only she knew someone in Chicago, she could send a telegram to find out.

She got up from her chair, realized that she'd been sitting on a couple of magazines, and picked them up. The topmost magazine was *China's Millions,* from the CIM, and a short notice caught her eye. "Mr. and Mrs. Isaac Page have been transferred to the Chicago area. . . ."

She reread the paragraph in amazement. The Pages—of course! She'd known them for years, and Mr. Page was a good friend of her father's. As a little girl she had loved his jokes and fun, and she had always called him Daddy Page. And now the Pages were in Chicago, still working for the CIM! They would know about Moody. She hurried off to send the telegram and soon had a reply. YES, INDEED. THE INSTITUTE EVEN HAS AN EMPLOYMENT BUREAU TO

HELP YOU FIND APPROPRIATE WORK. HOPING TO SEE YOU. ISAAC PAGE.

By Monday morning, Isobel's letter of resignation was in the mail and she had started on her application papers to Moody. "Yes, I'm sure," she told her curious friends. "I know this is what God wants me to do."

He had provided the miracle that changed Mother's mind. He had allowed her to write to the school board in time. He had given her the information about students working at Moody. How could she wonder?

The last weeks of summer sped by, although they were filled with increasing turmoil. Mother had changed her mind. "But you said I could go, and I've already resigned my job," Isobel reminded her.

"But you're my only daughter," Mother kept saying. "It's such a silly, romantic idea to want to bury yourself on the mission field. Why don't you get a nice Christian job here in Vancouver?"

Isobel tried to reason with her, aching at the thought of leaving her mother in this state of mind. And she wondered what to do about her lack of money.

Her train ticket to Chicago was paid for, thanks to Marjorie, but she didn't have any money for food along the way. She'd used every extra cent to help pay off the family's debts that had piled up when her father's mining investments failed.

Well, she thought, it won't hurt me to eat lightly for a couple of days. And the Lord knows all about Mother.

She encouraged herself with a remark that J. O. Fraser had made at The Firs last summer: "You must not pity me—Christ has promised, *Verily I say unto you, There is no man that hath left house, or brethren, or sisters, or mother . . . for my sake and the gospel's, but he shall receive an hundredfold in this time . . . and in the world to come eternal life.*"

Quietly she made all the arrangements necessary for taking a long trip and enrolling in a new school; then she waited.

Chapter Three

By the time Isobel boarded the train and was speeding across the continent, she had received a surprising amount of money. A gift had come from J. O. Fraser himself, and at the train station, many friends handed her small envelopes, each with a few dollars inside. The gifts added up to enough for her meals with a little left over, and she gratefully tucked away the extra money for emergencies.

As soon as she saw a sign for Chicago and the train began to slow, she pinned her dark, fine hair back into place and tried to smooth out her wrinkled skirt. She repacked her suitcase. Then she sat and fidgeted while they rattled past cluttered alleys and drab grey buildings.

At last the train slid to a stop and its doors jerked open. She shuffled along with the other passengers into the vast waiting room of the station, wondering what to do next. Then she caught sight of a familiar face: Daddy Page. How wonderful to see his beaming face—how good of him to meet her!

He steered her to his car, and as they drove through the windswept streets, she told him about her trip, and how the Lord had provided food money at the last minute, how faithful He had been, and—

"Well, here we are," Daddy Page said. Isobel fell silent as they parked in front of soaring grey buildings. She tipped her head back to stare up at the rows of lighted windows. Here she was indeed! The Lord had really done it.

After she had registered, Daddy Page was there again to take her out for an ice-cream soda and hear how the Lord had brought her to Moody. Nine years ago, Isobel remembered, before Daddy Page and his wife left for China, he had put a hand on her shoulder and said, "Isobel, I am going to pray that God will send you to China."

Back then, she had no intention of becoming a missionary, and her first thought had been, *You mean thing!*

Now, as she swirled a spoon through her soda, she thought, I'm glad he kept praying. She launched into a vivid description of her university experiences and her meeting with J. O. Fraser. Then she told him about her hopes of working with the Lisu. Daddy Page had tears in his eyes as he listened.

She thought of another incident to report. "Today when I lined up to register, I found out that we have to pay our first month's fees in advance. But the Lord already knew. Remember I told you about those last-minute gifts at the train station? Well, I had some money left over, and it was just enough. My school bill is all paid up now until Marjorie's money comes."

She smiled contentedly at Daddy Page, and he smiled back, as if he understood how marvelous it was to see the Lord provide for unexpected needs. Oh, it was good to be able to talk to him, here in this huge city where she didn't know anyone else!

Before long, though, Isobel had a problem to share with him. "I found out that I won't be allowed to work until the second term," she confided one day. It didn't surprise her when Daddy Page remarked, "Well, we'll have to pray about that."

She didn't tell him that she'd been depending on getting a job so she could buy some warm winter clothes; Chicago, with its biting north wind, would be much colder than Vancouver. She had decided to imitate Hudson Taylor: she would talk to the Lord and no one else about her need for a winter coat.

A few days later, Daddy Page called to see her. "Let's go," he said. "I've got permission from the dean to take you around the corner and have you meet someone."

Isobel joined him in a short walk down the street, wondering if this was one of his jokes. Daddy Page paused at the door of a bank, marched in, and introduced her to the manager. What was he doing? It looked as if he were opening a bank account. For her. And in it he deposited a hundred dollars!

"Oh, thank you, but I can't take your money—"

Gently he stopped her. "Your father has given me and mine as much as this and more in years gone past," he said. "This is just a small return to him."

It wasn't until they stepped out of the bank, back into the blustering wind, that Isobel realized the significance of Daddy Page's gift. A warm coat! she thought joyfully. God is going to take care of me—just like Hudson Taylor.

She soon settled into the busy routine of student life: classes, meals, meetings, homework. Her roommate was a girl she had met at The Firs, and she was delighted to have a friend like Billie during those first homesick days among hundreds of strangers. She and Billie could pray together and study together, and best of all, they could walk down to the huge, noisy dining room together.

Meals were served family style, with a senior and junior student sitting at each end of the table. The other students took turns bringing hot food from the kitchen, getting seconds, and clearing away the dishes. One evening as Isobel waited in line for the hot vegetables, she daydreamed about finally getting to China. Two more years of this, she thought.

As she turned, she looked into the blue eyes of another dreamer. For an instant she couldn't move, then she glanced away. The owner of those blue eyes was the student who ran the dishwasher. She snatched up a bowl of vegetables and hurried back to the table, annoyed to find herself wondering who he was.

Don't think about him, she told herself. Keep your mind on China. But every time she went back to the kitchen, she couldn't help looking to see if he was there.

In the weeks that followed, Isobel resisted her impulse to ask about the blue-eyed stranger, and she plunged into her training with vigor. She listened carefully during the classes in Bible analysis and took plenty of notes, thinking they might come in handy. In music class she learned how to conduct and to sing in parts. The singing reminded her of J. O. Fraser and his stories of the Lisu's beautiful singing. Someday, perhaps, she would be there to hear it.

Besides her classes, she found plenty to keep her on the run: meetings to attend, friends to pray with, warm clothes to sew. And at mealtime, she helped to bring the food or clear the table, as everyone else did.

Sometimes she had to carry dishes back into the kitchen, and she had to walk right past *him,* the blue-eyed dishwasher. She found herself wondering whether he had asked about the girl who wore the green blouse trimmed in brown. He probably knew her name and everything about her. At least he didn't speak; she was glad of that. It did seem, though, that she kept running into him at the Student Volunteer Prayer Band. And when she decided to join the small group that met to talk about missions in China, there he was again.

When Isobel's turn came to bring a devotional at the Prayer Band, she decided to talk about fellowship with God. To help herself and her listeners establish a definite prayer time each day, she wrote out a simple pledge. Anyone who signed it would try to have at least one hour of devotions each day during the school year.

I have to plan my day, Isobel thought. She would split the hour into thirty minutes, morning and evening. Morning was the hardest. Part of her assigned work at Moody was to set tables in the dining room at 6:30 A.M., so she tried getting up at 5:00 A.M. Not very sturdy and already thin, she began losing too much weight, so she decided on 5:30 A.M. That time worked out well, except that it disturbed her sleeping roommate. Slowly she walked down the long dormitory hall, wondering what to do.

A few days later, her roommate said, "I shouldn't have made such a fuss about having the light on in the morning—where do you disappear to?"

"Oh, there's a big closet down the hall with a light in it. I go there for my quiet time."

Her roommate raised an eyebrow. "The cleaning closet? There's nowhere to sit."

"I just turn over one of those nice big scrub buckets," Isobel said.

"Isobel Miller, if you aren't something! How can you stand it with all those mops and dust rags hanging over your head?"

She smiled. "I don't notice them. Really, it's fine."

Each student was required to do a Practical Christian Work assignment, and Isobel dreaded finding out what hers would be. She knew that working in the crowded streets and tenements of Chicago would be valuable experience, but she had always been timid about soulwinning.

When she finally reported to the Practical Christian Work office, she was dismayed to find out that she would be working in one of Chicago's slum districts. But her worry eased as soon as she met her senior partner, petite Ethel Thompson—"Tommy"—whom everybody loved for her Southern drawl and her ready sense of humor.

Tommy started by telling Isobel about the poverty-stricken Italian quarter where they'd be visiting and teaching Sunday school. It was difficult work, but she'd found that the more they prayed, the more God blessed. Isobel remembered J. O. Fraser's teaching about the weapon of prayer, and she suggested that they meet every day to pray about their project. Tommy's eyes brightened, and she agreed with enthusiasm.

Each day they prayed together for half an hour before noon, and each week they climbed dark, broken stairways and trudged down hallways that reeked of filth. One person, then another, listened to their message, and during the next few months, Isobel saw God change the lives of several adults and many children.

One day Isobel was invited to a surprise birthday party for Daddy Page. When she found out that male students would be there, she almost changed her mind about going. She had decided not to do any dating at Moody, remembering her heartache over Ben. Fortunately, the Vancouver boy whom Mother liked so well had decided to go to another school. Everything was simpler if she just stayed away from parties.

But this was Daddy Page's birthday! Finally she agreed, and her group of girls set off to catch the 7:30 P.M. streetcar. While they waited on the corner of Clark Street, the young men arrived. The leader of the girls' group made introductions. "This is Jack Graham, and John Kuhn, and . . ." But Isobel had stopped listening; she was looking into the face of the blue-eyed dishwasher. John Kuhn.

It turned out to be a wonderful party, and in the following weeks, Moody's kitchen proved to be a good place for Isobel and John to get acquainted. Finally, one evening while Isobel stood in the kitchen filling a teapot with hot water, John asked her for a date. She agreed, not without misgivings. But she found that her long days of work and study were lightened by the happiness of her times with John.

Chapter Four

Before long it was December, almost the end of Isobel's first term at school. Over the months she had thought often about her family and prayed that the Lord would change her mother's heart. Mother had sent plenty of newsy letters, but no word of encouragement.

One day a letter from her mother mentioned that she had a tumor. The doctor had said she must either have surgery or take a series of treatments, and she was trying to decide what to do. Isobel prayed that God would give her mother wisdom, and she shared her heavy heart with her roommate and her prayer group.

The next thing she knew, a telegram had arrived from her father. He tried to give her the bad news gently, but it was still a shock. Mother had chosen surgery and had died in the hospital after the operation. The funeral would be over before she could get home, Father said, so she should probably just stay at school.

Isobel poured out her grief to the Lord. Mother *gone?* How could life go on without her concern, her affection, her being there? Even her opposition to Isobel's plans had been rooted in love; she hadn't wanted to give up her only daughter.

Memories haunted Isobel's days and nights: Mother walking with them on the beach; Mother reading to them in the evening;

Mother playing the piano while they sang. And Mother's bitter comment resounded through her mind: *"If you go to China, it will be over my dead body."*

"Oh, Lord," she cried, "why did it have to be this way?"

Much later, Isobel learned that the night before her mother died, she had written to an old friend with regret, remarking that her busy life's work now seemed useless. Then she had concluded, "I feel that my little girl has chosen the better part in wishing to devote all her life to the Lord."

Isobel's eyes filled with tears as she read those words. God had answered her prayer in His own time; at the last minute, He had changed Mother's heart. And He had made it possible for her to go to China with her mother's blessing.

During the Christmas holidays, she took a job as waitress in a nearby restaurant, and when school began again in January, she continued to work part-time. Only a few weeks into the term, she was called out of class to the Dean of Women's office. Another telegram had arrived from home: FATHER FATALLY INJURED IN ELEVATOR ACCIDENT. COME HOME AT ONCE. MURRAY.

No, cried Isobel silently. Not again! J. O. Fraser's warning flashed through her mind. Was Satan trying to get her away from Bible school?

She closed her eyes, then opened them quickly, realizing that she was still in the Dean of Women's office. The dean was leaning across her desk, looking concerned. "Isobel, who is Murray?"

"My brother." And Murray had been bitterly opposed to her plans.

"Is there anything I can do for you? Anyone I can call?"

"Yes." Steadied by the memory of her talk with J. O. Fraser, she was able to answer quietly. "Yes, please. I would like to talk to Dr. Isaac Page."

By the time Daddy Page arrived, Isobel had decided on a plan. "Mr. Fraser told me that something like this might happen," she said. "I'll start packing. But could you send a telegram to Mr. Charles Thompson, the CIM secretary in Vancouver? He can find out if my father is as badly injured as Murray said."

Before supper time that evening, Isobel had an answering telegram. FATHER IMPROVING SENDS LOVE AND SAYS STAY AT YOUR POST. WRITING. THOMPSON.

Isobel stared at the telegram in her hand. How could Mr. Fraser have known that something like this would happen? His relationship with God must have been so deep and so real that God's Spirit could tell him to warn her. If only she could know God that well!

Mr. Thompson's letter, following soon after, gave details of the accident. Her father had been riding in an elevator that dropped four stories to a cement basement floor. The crash had caused some injuries, but he would survive. As Isobel sat down to begin a letter home, she thanked God again for His guidance. No matter what it took, she would make sure she was ready for Him to use in China.

She returned to her studies, her waitressing jobs, and her Christian work assignment with new energy. Waitressing was a constant drain on her time and her health, but she had no choice if she was going to have enough money for next year. As it was, she had barely enough money for essentials.

When her missions teacher, Dr. Glover, told the class about the Foreign Missions Convention in Washington, D.C., and urged students to sign up as delegates, Isobel knew there was no way she could afford it. But oh, how she wanted to go! Famous missionaries and native Christians would be visiting from all over the world. President Coolidge would be there to open the conference. And John Kuhn was going too.

"There's only a week left to sign up," Dr. Glover announced one day. "And we have room for one more delegate." Isobel had felt all week that the Lord meant for her to go. But how? She didn't have a cent to spare for the conference. Maybe the Lord would send her a big check in the mail. But no money came, and on the last day she began to wonder whether she had been a victim of her own wishful thinking.

That day at noon, there were no letters in her mailbox, nothing but a note: "Call at Dr. Glover's office immediately." In breathless haste she ran through the snow to the main building and knocked at his door. Dr. Glover invited her in with a broad smile. A certain lady who wished to remain unknown had offered to send her to the missionary conference. The lady would provide money for everything—train fare, hotel, meals—and even an extra twenty dollars for spending money. "Can you be ready to leave by tomorrow morning?" he asked.

Could she! Isobel ran back to her room, told her roommate over and over about the wonderful thing God had done, and began to pack her suitcase with joyous haste.

The missions conference proved to be all that she had dreamed of and more. She and the seven other delegates talked with missionary speakers, went sightseeing together, and formed friendships that were to last the rest of their lives.

Since John Kuhn was one of the conference delegates, it was also a good time for getting to know him better. Isobel found that they had much in common, and during the months that followed, she enjoyed his company more and more. They double-dated with their friends Francis and Jennie, taking hilarious trips in the two boys' ramshackle car named Jennybelle. They also spent quiet moments together in prayer, joining with other students who wanted to be missionaries in China.

But Isobel was determined not to rush ahead; she had to be sure about John. Why might she want to marry him? It couldn't be his deep blue eyes; it couldn't be his calm, steady temperament, so different from hers. It couldn't be that he wanted to go to China too, or that they shared the same desire for God's highest purpose in their lives.

She had to be sure that John Kuhn was God's man for her. She didn't have that assurance, so when John graduated from Moody in the spring of 1926, there was no definite commitment between them. But after he left, she spent many hours writing to him, and she often went out of her way to check her mailbox for his replies.

Meanwhile, through her waitressing work and gifts from friends and strangers, Isobel managed to keep up with her school bills. She had spent her first summer visiting an aunt in Canada, but the second summer she stayed in Chicago to work. Since she missed a term of school because of sickness, her last term at Moody was the fall of 1926. The weeks slipped by in a blur of work and study, and her needs, both physical and spiritual, seemed overwhelming at times.

In October 1926, John Kuhn sailed for China as a member of the China Inland Mission, and that December Isobel graduated from Moody. In her mind's eye she could already see herself climbing the rugged western mountains where the Lisu tribe lived. But how long would it take her to get there?

Chapter Five

ANTI-FOREIGN UPRISINGS IN CHINA, shouted the newspaper headlines. MOBS SEIZE BRITISH CONCESSION.

Isobel read the article impatiently, wishing there was some good news from China for a change. All the CIM missionaries had been forced to draw back to the city of Shanghai, on China's coast. John had been living in the training home at Anking and had to take a dangerous boat trip down to Shanghai, but he was safe. Everyone was praying for J. O. Fraser and the other missionaries who were still deep in the interior of China.

She sighed. With China in such a turmoil, the Mission might not send out any new missionaries for a while. She had almost finished candidate school at the CIM home in Toronto, and she'd hoped to get out to China soon. Did this mean a long delay?

Slowly she folded up the newspaper. Right now she had something more worrisome to think about. This afternoon she was to meet the Council; they would ask her questions about her desire to be a missionary, and she would have to do her best to answer them, even though she wasn't good at thinking on her feet.

She found that meeting with the Council wasn't as bad as she had feared, and that evening she went to hear their decision with a light heart. Mr. Brownlee, who was in charge of the Toronto

Mission Home, told her first that the Council was quite satisfied with her answers and her conduct while in school. He paused, and Isobel wondered at the grave expression on his face. "But the Council has asked me to speak to you about a serious matter."

He told her that one of the six people who sent in letters of recommendation had not given her a good report. The person had written that Isobel was proud, disobedient, and likely to be a troublemaker. Mr. Brownlee continued, "I want to explain to you how these characteristics can cause some terrible problems on the mission field."

For the next hour, kindly and thoroughly, he talked to her. And Isobel tried to listen, even though her mind was racing and her cheeks burned with embarrassment. At last he concluded. "The Council will accept you conditionally. Since we cannot send out any new missionaries for a while, we will wait and see if you can conquer these tendencies. If you can, you will be accepted fully, and you will be sent out with the first group of new missionaries that goes to China."

Isobel stumbled out of the room and crept upstairs to her bedroom. Slowly, mechanically, she prepared for bed, and all through an endless night the accusations paraded through her mind. *Proud—disobedient—a troublemaker.* Who could have said that about her? Of course the CIM would never tell.

Disobedient? That criticism seemed especially unfair. At Moody she'd been careful, as a matter of honor, to obey every little rule, even the ones that seemed unreasonable. Even the ones that the other students didn't bother obeying.

And now, she thought miserably, what am I to do? The way to China is closed, at least for now. The only thing that's left is to go home to Vancouver and ask the Lord to use me there.

During the long train trip across Canada to British Columbia, Isobel thought about what had happened, and she wrote to some of her friends, describing the incident. When she arrived in Vancouver, she agreed to keep house for her father and her brother, still wondering dismally what kind of work the Lord wanted her to do.

Before long, sympathetic letters arrived from her friends. But one letter was different. "What surprised me most of all was your attitude in this matter," wrote Roy Bancroft. "You sound bitter and resentful. Why, if anyone had said to me 'Roy B., you are proud, disobedient, and a troublemaker,' I would answer: 'Amen, brother! And even then you haven't said the half of it!' What good thing is there in any of us, anyway? We have victory in these things only as we bring them one by one to the Cross. . . ."

Oh, Roy, you're right! Isobel thought. She fell to her knees and asked the Lord for a different attitude. Bitter and resentful? It was true; she would never make a good missionary as long as she felt that way. She resolved to watch carefully that no pride, no disobedience, no rebellion would have any place in her life.

Sometime later, quite by accident, she found out who had sent the accusing letter to the CIM. The writer was a former teacher who had asked her to spy on the students in the class. Isobel had refused, feeling that it was an unworthy thing to do, and inadvertently she had made an enemy.

Her first thought was to write the Mission and explain the background of that bad reference. Then, remembering Roy's words, she changed her mind. Why try to convince the Mission that she was perfect? All too soon they would find out what she was really like. She dropped her notepaper into a drawer and shut it firmly. The Lord had been remarkably kind to let her find out who had written that letter; she wouldn't let it bother her anymore.

One day Isobel was asked to speak at a meeting of the Vancouver Girls Corner Club, a group of young Christian businesswomen who had joined together to evangelize the career girls of Vancouver. A week later, the club president asked her to become their superintendent, and after praying about it, Isobel accepted the position. Her job was to encourage the girls, speak at meetings, and plan outings.

Although she still dreaded getting up in front of strangers, she enjoyed working and praying with the club members and their friends. When she noticed that some of the girls had singing ability, she organized a quartet and trained them so well that they were asked to sing in churches all over Vancouver. It turned out to be a good way to reach large numbers of career girls for Christ.

Isobel's activities with the girls kept her busy, but through all her days beat a pulse of longing for China. The small house she shared with her father and brother looked out toward the Pacific ocean, and sometimes she stood on the front porch watching the deep blue swells of the harbor. Those same waves lap the shores of China, she thought. Often, as she went about her work, she looked up at the cloud-wreathed mountains behind Vancouver and wondered, Are the mountains in Lisu country as tall and grand as these?

The newspapers still carried accounts of fighting between the Nationalist and Communist armies in China. On the other hand, reports from the Mission indicated that the Chinese seemed to be growing more tolerant toward foreigners. Isobel kept her ears open for any scraps of information about China, and she eagerly read the letters from her friends in Shanghai.

Meanwhile, wonderful letters came from John. She knew that he wanted to marry her, but still she held back from an engagement. It looked as if the Mission was going to assign him to Kansu, a province in China's far northwest, and she knew God had called her to the Lisu tribes in Yunnan Province. She would wait and see where the Mission sent him before making up her mind.

At last John sent the all-important news. He had been assigned to the tribes of Yunnan Province. Would Isobel go there as his wife? She was to send her answer by cable: Light for yes and Dark for no.

Isobel spread out his letter before the Lord, just to be sure; then joyously she sent the cable: *LIGHT!*

She followed with a letter telling John about the verse God had given her in Matthew, chapter 6. *Seek ye first the kingdom of God, and his righteousness; and all these things shall be added unto you.* Could they make GOD FIRST the motto for their life together?

By this time the news from China had improved, and after more than a year of waiting, it looked as if the door for new missionaries was opening at last. In the spring of 1928, the CIM accepted Isobel unconditionally and scheduled her to sail for China in October. The director took one look at her pale, tired face and ordered her to resign from the Corner Club and take six months to rest.

Rest, yes; that is a good idea, Isobel thought, but how can I afford to take six months off? She was wondering what to do when Mr. and Mrs. Whipple invited her to spend the summer with them at The Firs. She could help—cleaning the cabins and getting things ready for camp—but first she was to have a whole month to herself.

She accepted their offer gladly, thinking how wonderful it would be to join the Whipples' large family once more. Her bedroom was a converted upstairs porch surrounded by tall fir trees that screened it and filled the air with fragrance. During that first month, it seemed like sheer luxury to sleep as late as she wanted and to have plenty of time for prayer at her favorite spot among the trees.

When the Conference opened, she was ready to throw all her energies into working with the campers. She found it a unique experience to join Mrs. Whipple in prayer for the girls and to share her desire that each one would yield to the Lord before she went home. Many of the girls were as confused and needy as Isobel once had been, and she rejoiced with Mrs. Whipple to see God at work in their lives.

As her summer at The Firs came to a close, Isobel began to think about the equipment she would need to take to China. For one thing, she didn't even have enough money to get back to Vancouver. But a gift from her brother, Murray, provided her fare home, and when she arrived, John's letter waited with another surprise. Fifty dollars! He wanted to have a share in her field equipment, he wrote, but she could use the money for any need.

The Lord provided the rest of her equipment through gifts from friends and showers from the Corner Club. Remembering that the Lisu loved music, Isobel decided to take along her guitar and to use some of the money to buy a small portable organ. She called it her "baby organ."

A crowd of friends—many of them Corner Club girls—gathered at the wharf in Vancouver Harbour to see her off. Isobel leaned over the ship's railing. Hebrews 6:1, the verse she had used to challenge her girls, was still on her mind, and she called, "Let us go on!"

Tear-stained faces lit up and hands waved back, so she knew they had heard. The ship's anchors rattled, the bright paper streamers stretched and tore, and the *Empress of Russia* steamed away from the wharf.

They stopped briefly at Victoria on Vancouver Island, and there Isobel's father gave her a final hug and said good-bye. As the ship headed out toward the Pacific Ocean, Isobel stayed at the railing, and soon the purser brought her a telegram: WE WILL GO ON—YOUR CORNER CLUB GIRLS. She smiled through a haze of tears. Yes, the Lord would faithfully lead her girls. And He would lead her too.

The ocean breeze caught her long brown hair as she lifted her chin and gazed across the water. To China. To the Lisu. And to John.

Chapter Six

Among the missionaries on Isobel's ship were several young women and one veteran, Miss Ruth Paxson. When the group begged Miss Paxson to give them an hour's Bible teaching each day, she agreed.

She had just finished writing *Life on the Highest Plane,* and she taught them its basic ideas, using examples from her own wealth of experience. She also discussed the problems and temptations of missionary life. One statement in particular made Isobel stop and think. "Girls," Miss Paxson said quietly, "when you get to China, all the scum of your nature will rise to the top."

Isobel glanced at the earnest faces of the girls around her. Scum? she wondered. Wasn't that a strong expression to use with this group? But she filed the comment away in her mind and then forgot about it in the excitement of arriving in China and getting started on language study.

She gave herself wholeheartedly to the new language and culture during her first year of language school. Kunming, the city in which she lived, wasn't in Lisu country, but at least it was the capital of Yunnan Province. She could look toward the western edge of Yunnan and dream about the Lisu who lived in those far-off mountain ranges. And John was stationed a short distance down the railroad at the little town of Chengchiang, close enough for visiting.

She and John were required by the Mission to wait for a year before they could marry; so they made their plans and waited as patiently as they could. The date was set for November 14, 1929, but two weeks before the wedding they had to change it to November 4 so the American consul could be present. Isobel sent a runner to John in Chengchiang, hoping that the earlier date would work out for him, and to her delight, he answered by coming himself.

Soon they were making new plans. In the midst of their discussion the smile faded from John's face. "Oh—the wedding ring!" he exclaimed. "I left it in Chengchiang." Isobel assured him that they could borrow another one temporarily, but they both knew it wouldn't be the same. The next day when John's cook-boy, Yin-chang, arrived with the baggage, she was glad to hear that he had found the ring in John's drawer and brought it with him.

Isobel had hoped for a wedding with few guests, but she soon learned that the white community in Kunming regarded any Western wedding as a social affair. Not wanting to offend anyone, she ended up inviting all the Westerners in Kunming.

When the long-awaited day came, Isobel and John were married in a Chinese church made beautiful by flowers and greenery. Then, thanks to a gift from John's father, they rode off in rickshas for a week's stay at the luxurious French hotel. After their honeymoon, they moved to Chengchiang to begin life among the country Chinese.

John had found a place for them to live, and Isobel could hardly wait to see it. She followed him down a street that was crowded with dingy shops, rickshas, and barking dogs that ran between baskets of vegetables and crates of quacking ducks.

Then he turned and climbed up a few steps. "Only two rooms— I told you it wasn't much," he said, sounding anxious. "No, there aren't any windows, but any time you want to see out—" He rolled back the folding doors that made up the front and back walls, and Isobel was immediately conscious of the people that thronged the busy street: housewives on errands, shopkeepers, chestnut vendors, children, beggars.

She stepped back. Anyone walking by could see right into their rooms. But—she glanced over her shoulder—with the folding doors closed, it would be like living in a wooden box.

"Here's the kitchen," John was saying, and she followed him out to a verandah with a charcoal stove at one end. Nearby were two small rooms for Yin-chang and his new wife.

Isobel set out to make their two rooms as attractive as possible. Blue and white for the bedroom, she decided, and brown and green for the living room. With their wedding gift money, they bought wicker furniture and a matching beige rug to cover the warped floorboards. Her trunk, spread with a pretty green and crimson traveling rug, could go in one corner, and John's table-desk would look fine in the other corner. On the wall she hung their motto: GOD FIRST.

Her first guests were Chinese peasant women who had come to market. They trooped up the stairs, chattering happily and exclaiming over Isobel's living room. Isobel knew that it must seem quite grand, compared with their dark huts. Eagerly she began to talk about the gospel, trying out her limited Chinese. They seemed to understand!

But look at that old woman over in the corner. She had blown her nose with her fingers; now she was wiping her hand on the traveling rug. Isobel tried to collect her thoughts and go on. Suddenly one young mother jumped up. Laughing, she held her baby son out away from herself and headed for the doorway, leaving a soiled wet streak across the new brown rug.

Isobel reminded herself that the woman was used to a mud floor, and quietly finished her talk. But when her guests finally left, she stood in the living room and stared resentfully at the wet streak on her cherished rug. The motto on the wall caught her eye: GOD FIRST. A question rang through her mind: what was going to come first—an attractive living room for her? Or a room to share with the Chinese people?

"Oh, Lord," she cried, "make this room yours!" She offered to God all the new furniture, the rug, and every *thing* she possessed—to be used however He wanted.

During the next few days, Isobel thought often about the advice Miss Paxson had given them during the voyage to China. She already knew that the thousands of Chinese peasants who farmed the plains around Chengchiang were poor. But she was learning firsthand that poverty meant no washing machines and no hot baths with soap. It meant mud floors, one set of clothes, and *bugs.*

Whenever she went visiting, it seemed that fleas jumped up from the mud floors to greet her and lice crawled into her hair. Flies and mosquitoes buzzed around her face and arms and legs, although they never bothered John.

She really did want to reach these people for the Lord. But sometimes when she went to put an arm around a country woman, all she could think of was the bedbugs, or the fleas, or the lice. *The scum of your nature,* Miss Paxson had said. What in the world was she going to do?

She took her problem to the Lord, and He gave her Galatians 2:8. *For he that wrought effectually in Peter . . . the same was mighty in me.* Isobel applied it to her need for victory over the things that bothered her. "Lord, make these souls more important to me than anything else," she prayed, and in answer to that prayer, her attitude gradually changed.

Missionary friends gave her some practical tips for coping with the differences in her new life. Insect powder, for one thing, helped with the ever-present creeping and flying creatures. And when a Chinese hostess proudly served the chunks of glistening white fat that Isobel could hardly eat, the family dog scavenging under the table could help her to quietly dispose of her share.

Bean curd was another matter. To Isobel, bean curd looked like squares of grey flannel cloth, and she declared that it tasted like boiled flannel too. She managed to eat it when they were out visiting among the Chinese, but she began to notice that it was appearing more and more frequently in the meals that Yin-chang cooked for them. Why did they have to eat bean curd when she'd seen baskets of potatoes and carrots and onions at the market?

John had taken charge of the housekeeping for those first months so she could keep up with her language study, and she went to him. "Please make sure that Yin-chang buys some potatoes and carrots," she pleaded. "Something I can eat."

John gave the order, but sure enough, that night when Isobel looked hungrily at the steaming bowls Yin-chang was arranging on the table, all she saw was rice with meat and those grey flannel squares of bean curd. Of course bean curd was easier for Yin-chang and his wife to fix, since potatoes and carrots had to be peeled, and clearly, Yin-chang preferred bean curd.

Timidly she asked, "But the potatoes and carrots—where are they?"

Yin-chang and his wife exchanged a glance. "Oh, we didn't see them today when we went to the market," he said.

"Don't we have anything else to eat?"

Yin-chang and his wife shook their heads. "No, nothing."

Isobel, exhausted from a long day of visiting from farm to farm, sank onto her bed; she felt the tears rising and couldn't hold them back. Finally she fell asleep, only to waken near midnight, shaky with hunger.

"Won't you try a little rice?" asked John, looking anxious. "I'll get Yin-chang to heat some up for you."

For his sake she ate the rice that Yin-chang brought, even though a mound of bean curd steamed on top of it. After that, strangely enough, bean curd never seemed quite as repulsive.

The problem of Yin-chang's laziness had not been solved, however, and it kept prickling into Isobel's life. One cold day as she shivered over her language lessons with her Chinese teacher, she gazed suspiciously at their tiny charcoal brazier. It held only a few feebly burning coals. What had Yin-chang done with the new, much larger charcoal brazier? She soon discovered Yin-chang and his wife back in their bedroom, enjoying the warmth of hot coals piled high on the new brazier.

What a pair of rascals, she thought, and she bit her tongue to keep back the sharp words. Even though Yin-chang hurried to bring her the larger brazier, Isobel decided that she and John had better have another discussion about his cook-boy. Yin-chang had not always been like this, John was quick to point out. But he had to admit that the cook-boy had changed since he'd been married.

Yin-chang's wife had a pretty face, but her selfish nature soon showed up, and it became obvious that she was not a true Christian; she had probably joined the church to please her family. She often influenced Yin-chang to take advantage of his former comradeship with John, but even so, it was hard for John to consider dismissing them.

Daily incidents of carelessness, and sulking, and "borrowing" of such things as Isobel's perfume finally brought her to the boiling point. One day after yet another incident in which John sided with Yin-chang, she snatched up her coat and hat and stalked out of the house.

Down the street and out the west gate she marched. How awful it had been to see that smirk on Yin-chang's face! A fine thing it was when your own husband refused to correct a lazy servant! On and on she went, following the road that wandered across a wide plain dotted with villages. There was no place to sit unobserved; no trees, no hills; nothing but fields and people.

Hours later as she passed through yet another village, she realized that the Chinese were eyeing her curiously. Dusk was beginning to fall. What was a respectable woman doing alone on the road at this time of day?

Isobel slowed her pace, suddenly aware that her behavior might make it harder to reach these people for Christ. "Lord, I'm sorry," she prayed. "I was just thinking about my hurt feelings, and I forgot about You. I've been a terrible witness. What do you want me to do?"

Right away she knew the answer: she should go back. But how could she go back and watch those servants laugh at her humiliation? No, she had to do it. She turned and plodded toward home, scolding herself. Why hadn't she said anything to the Lord before about this servant problem? She'd tried to manage it on her own, and look what had happened.

All during the long, weary trip back, she talked to God about Yin-chang and his wife—how careless and rude they'd become, and how John didn't seem to notice. It was getting dark as she dragged herself up the steps to their two small rooms. She paused in the doorway. What should she do now? Well, she had asked the Lord to take charge of the situation; she'd wait and see.

John glanced up from his desk in the corner, relief spreading across his face. To his anxious questions she said only that she'd gone for a walk. Yin-chang heated up her supper, Isobel ate it quietly, and they spent the rest of the evening studying Chinese as usual.

But that night, after their bedtime Bible reading and prayer, John told her that she could dismiss Yin-chang and his wife if she wanted to. Then he warned her that good servants were hard to find. Isobel didn't let herself worry about that. How wonderfully God had worked in her husband's heart!

"Oh, thank you!" she exclaimed to John. "I know it will be hard on you to lose Yin-chang, but we'll manage!" And she began making plans to do the work herself if necessary. Anything was better than what had happened that day.

Chapter Seven

The next weeks were more difficult than Isobel could have imagined. Yin-chang and his wife did not go willingly, and once they left, housework took up most of Isobel's time.

Preparing meals meant bargaining in the market each day for meat and vegetables since they had no refrigerator and then struggling to light their primitive Chinese stove. Doing laundry meant hauling the water up from a well, heating it, scrubbing the clothes by hand, and then hanging them to dry over the verandah railing. Even with John's help, it seemed that she could never spend as much time as she wanted to on language study.

As one weary day faded into the next, Isobel and John pleaded with the Lord to send them a good servant, and when He answered, He sent them one of the best. Mrs. Chang had been deserted by her husband and she needed a job; she proved to be a wonderfully capable and efficient helper. Although she was not a Christian, working and talking with Isobel drew her to the message of the gospel, and one day she accepted Christ as her Savior.

In all the excitement of settling into their first station, Isobel and John had not forgotten about the Lisu. The time at Chengchiang began to lengthen—six months, eight months—and in spite of their confidence that they were doing God's will, they began to wonder how long it might be before He would lead them into work with the mountain tribes.

One day as Isobel sat with her Chinese grammar, she lifted her head to watch a gilded sedan chair go by and saw John hurrying down the street. He dashed up the steps two at a time, waving a letter. It had to be good news. "From headquarters," he cried. "Our new appointment!"

"Where?"

"West—to Tali!"

Oh, thank you, Lord, thought Isobel. It's not exactly Lisu country, but it's in western Yunnan, and that's closer to the mountains than we've ever been before.

Quickly they checked the details. J. O. Fraser, now the director for Yunnan Province, wrote that they were to live in the old mission home at Tali and continue their language study. They would also help to establish the new missionaries who would be arriving. John was to preach in the districts around Tali and hunt for suitable houses that the newcomers would need when they began their own ministries.

Isobel enjoyed the next two and a half years at Tali. While John preached in the countryside, she kept on with her language study, taught a Bible class for Chinese women, and acted as hostess for missionaries and other Westerners who traveled through Tali. During that time, she and John welcomed ten new missionaries and helped them to get settled in nearby towns.

While they were working at Tali, they received an invitation from their missionary neighbors in Paoshan, ten days' journey to the west. Would Isobel and John come over and help with a special evangelistic outreach? Always eager to explore westward, Isobel and John accepted happily. Besides, Isobel could take her fourth oral Chinese language exam at Paoshan.

Their journey lay through the mountain ranges of western Yunnan, and it was a rougher trip than Isobel had ever experienced. Some of the rocky trails were so narrow that the travelers had to go single file: John first, on horseback or on foot; Isobel next in a *hwa-gan* (mountain chair); then their porters, Chinese coolies, with the baggage.

Riding in a mountain chair was the correct way for a woman to travel, but it took courage, Isobel discovered, especially when they were climbing up one of those slippery dirt paths. Two coolies, one in front and one in back, carried the shafts of the *hwa-gan;* as the climb grew steeper, the coolies began to grunt and the chair tilted back. When they turned a corner on the narrow trail, the coolies slowed, feeling for secure footing, and the chair swung right out over the side of the mountain. At first Isobel couldn't bear to look over the edge of the cliff. She wouldn't let herself think about what would happen if one of those coolies stumbled.

Although it was a tiresome way to travel, each day Isobel found new beauty in the wild mountainsides, and each night when they stopped at a dusty little inn, they had opportunities to speak of Christ.

It was from a high ridge, one day at sunset, that she first saw the valley of Yungping. Enclosed by towering mountains, its shimmering green fields threaded with a silver stream looked like something out of a fairy tale. She gazed at the scene, enthralled, until John waved her on and they started down a trail that dropped steeply for two thousand feet until it leveled out on the valley floor.

They stopped at a small market town for the night, and after supper they held an open-air meeting as usual. But the crowd, mostly Muslim, listened with cold indifference. This would be a discouraging place to work, Isobel thought. The next day they left Yungping and continued their trip, but she could not forget the lovely green valley with its difficult people.

Near the end of their first year in Tali, Isobel found out that they were going to have a baby. When she told John, his face lit up. "Wonderful!" he exclaimed. "Maybe it will be a boy. Then when the Chinese ask me 'Pastor Kuhn, have you any children?' I can say 'Yes, one, *hsiao tu-shu-ti.* (a small schoolboy).' "

"Oh," said Isobel, "but what if it's a girl—a 'cook-rice-to-eat' child?"

John just grinned at her; that would be wonderful too.

The nearest hospital was in Kunming, two weeks' journey to the east, so they decided to ask Miss Ling, a Chinese Christian nurse, to come and stay with them. In due time Miss Ling arrived, and so did the baby. Kathryn Alice-Ann Kuhn, named for her aunt Kathryn, was born on April 10, 1931. Soon afterwards, John took Isobel's hand and knelt by her bed to consecrate their daughter's life to the Lord. In this country where infants often died from unsanitary conditions or lack of medical help, Isobel was thankful that they could commit their baby's safekeeping to God.

It wasn't long before little Kathryn grew into a charming baby with sparkling hazel eyes and curly black eyelashes. Isobel didn't want her to be called by any of Aunt Kathryn's nicknames, so she made up one of her own: Rynna. To celebrate Rynna's one-month birthday, Isobel and John put on a feast for the Chinese, as was the custom. They gave her the Chinese name of Hong En (Vast Grace) and held a dedication service for her in the chapel at Tali.

By the time Kathryn was a year and a half old, Isobel and John had finished their language examinations, and the work was going well at Tali. In western Yunnan there were still hundreds of towns without a Christian witness, so they weren't surprised to receive a new assignment from J. O. Fraser. The letter said that they were to open up a work in the valley of Yungping.

Yungping! Isobel didn't mind the idea of moving. Wasn't Yungping farther west, closer to the Lisu? And it was a beautiful little valley. Away from the city of Tali, she wouldn't have as many Westerners to entertain, and she could spend more time with the people in the villages.

But she knew that the assignment discouraged John. The Muslims would be hard to reach, and he wouldn't be able to do the itinerant preaching that he enjoyed. For him, the prospect of working within the confines of one small valley seemed unbearable.

Shortly after they heard of the new assignment, Isobel was taken with a strange fever. Even the CIM nurse could not tell what it was, finally deciding that it must be some form of blackwater fever. But nothing seemed to help Isobel, and the nearest doctor was two weeks' journey away. As she grew steadily worse, John prayed desperately that her life would be spared. One night as he knelt by her bed, he surrendered his unwillingness to work in Yungping. The next day Isobel began to improve, and slowly she regained her health.

For their headquarters in Yungping they chose a little Chinese town called Old Market, located at the northern end of the valley. John found a house right on the edge of the river. It had three wings built around a small courtyard, and its fourth side, a crumbling wall, faced the water. Even though the house was dilapidated and needed a thorough cleaning, Isobel liked its many rooms and its privacy. A local carpenter agreed to put in a wooden floor, mend the roof, and straighten the walls. Isobel and a young helper attacked the age-old accumulation of dirt and cobwebs. The soot-encrusted upstairs room that had been the ancestral worship hall would be just right for their bedroom.

One afternoon, a delegation of town leaders came to visit, complete with gifts of sugar, tea, and a pair of bright red satin scrolls. The townsmen announced to John that they wanted to help him in his work. They had noticed that he did not drink liquor or use tobacco, and they had decided that the Christian church would be a modernizing influence on the town.

Isobel and John exchanged amazed glances; then, very carefully, John began to speak to them about Christ. At first the men nodded and smiled in agreement. Buddhism was old-fashioned; well, idols were old-fashioned too; yes, indeed, they said, Christianity was a fine, moral religion.

But when John explained that Christians could worship no one except God, they began to ask questions. What? Not worship the ancestors? No, John told them patiently, not even the ancestors, and he tried again to make the message of salvation clear to them. The townsmen began to edge their way toward the door. Surely Pastor Kuhn could not expect them to do that!

John thanked them for coming and encouraged them to return any time for more discussion. But he shook his head as they disappeared through the front gate. "Satan's first choice is to cooperate with us," he said, quoting from a book by G. Campbell Morgan. "Persecution is only his second-best method."

The work at Yungping turned out to be as difficult as John had feared. Isobel herself visited every village on the plain, speaking of God and His love to the women who lived in countless dusty courtyards. Her listeners, largely Muslim, were pathetically poor and could not read. A few believed, but only a handful, and those few were not strong enough to constitute a church.

As the discouraging months dragged into a new year, she began to wonder whether she and John would ever work with the Lisu. It had been ten years since God had first touched her heart with their needs, and here she was, still working with the Chinese. She had lived in China for five years and had finished all the necessary language examinations. Little Kathryn was old enough now to accompany them into the mountains. Why the delay? Soon they would be going home on furlough.

Each time she asked Mr. Fraser about joining the work, he said he didn't think she was physically strong enough to pioneer in the mountains. And each time he answered, she could see the vast Salween River Canyon with uncounted Lisu villages that had never heard of Christ—and only two missionaries, Leila and Allyn Cooke. Their needs were very real to her because she had learned all she could about the Lisu and prayed over every bit of news she heard.

Timidly she decided to try another request. The answer came back: "Wait until after your furlough. We will see then."

Isobel took her disappointment to the Lord, searching her heart at the same time. Perhaps He had never meant for her to work with the Lisu. Perhaps she had mistaken His direction. Very well; the one thing she wanted was to please Him. "I'm willing to stay here,

Lord—all my days," she said, "if only You will send *someone* to them."

The Lord gave her peace about the matter, and she turned back to her ministry with new contentment. Soon after, she realized that she wouldn't be able to work with the Lisu for a while anyway, since she and John were expecting another baby. She knew better than to take a newborn child pioneering into the mountains.

Late in that summer of 1933, John made a long survey trip into the western mountains while Isobel and three missionary girls carried on the ministry at Yungping. One afternoon the river that ran past their house began to rise. Soon it was lapping at their doorstep, and by evening its muddy waters swept into the downstairs rooms. Everyone in the house scrambled to move their things upstairs. Isobel did her best to help, even though there were some heavy trunks, and the next day she felt an unaccustomed pain. As the slow, agonizing days passed, she realized that she was going to lose their baby.

Oh, John, I need you! she cried. But there was no way to get in touch with him, and she felt as if she would drown in her pain and despair. When he finally arrived and learned of the miscarriage, he said the only thing that could console her. "God must have some purpose in this, dear. We will just ask Him what it is."

The next day they received a letter from J. O. Fraser. Not knowing what had happened to Isobel, he asked them to join in prayer about a problem that had arisen in the Lisu work. Two small Lisu churches in the Upper Salween Canyon were being persecuted because they would not grow opium. Leila and Allyn Cooke, the only missionaries in that region, had decided to separate so that each church would have a white missionary to take up their defense against the warlord who threatened them. Leila was staying with the church in the Oak Flat district, while Allyn took charge of the church at Luda, six days' journey to the north.

"I can't allow this to go on," wrote Mr. Fraser. "Leila Cooke is very brave to stay all alone in that isolated rough place, but I cannot allow husband and wife to continue in separation. Yet I have no one else to send."

John finished reading the letter, and Isobel's mind raced ahead to the solution. So this was how the Lord was going to work everything out! John looked at her and she smiled back, doubly comforted over their loss. With a newborn baby they could never have considered such a dangerous trip. She knew exactly how they were going to answer that letter.

Part II: The Steeps

1934-52

Chapter Eight

J. O. Fraser's reply to their letter was all that Isobel and John had prayed for. They were to make the trip into the Upper Salween Canyon, help Leila Cooke with the ministry at Oak Flat, and at the same time see whether Isobel could take the rough living conditions. While they were there, John could talk to the local officials about the opium problem.

Gratefully they made plans for the journey, and by March of 1934, everything was set. Two junior missionaries would temporarily take over the work in Yungping, and three-year-old Kathy would stay with them.

"I'll be gone for only a month, Rynna," Isobel whispered. Even so, tears stung her eyes as she gave Kathryn one last hug and they started on their journey.

For eight days they traveled northward up the valley of the Mekong River, spending the night in small towns along the way. Finally they reached the edge of the great mountain ranges that guard the Salween River. That night they slept in an old adobe farmhouse so filled with dust, cobwebs, and soot that they named it "The Dirtiest Inn in the World."

"It'll be a steep climb tomorrow," John told Isobel, "too steep for a mountain chair. But you'll love it when we get to the top. You'll be able to see all the way to the Salween mountains."

At dawn the next morning, Isobel awoke with all the symptoms of dysentery. "Probably some germ I picked up at the Dirtiest Inn in the World," she said grimly. "If we stay here, I'll surely catch something else. Get me up onto my horse, and I'll try to hang on."

They started off on a trail that zigzagged back and forth, up, and up again, climbing the steep flank of the mountain. At first they rode through groves of feathery, creaking bamboo, then they reached the pine trees that grew at higher altitudes. John called a halt at a deserted hut and made Isobel a cup of cocoa. She huddled over the fire, sipping the hot liquid and praying that it would stay down. It strengthened her, and she sat up a little straighter when John lifted her back onto her horse.

For the rest of the morning they climbed upward through immense trees hung with moss and tangled looping vines that shut out the sun. Isobel grew chilled and dizzy as she clung to her horse, but finally it lunged up onto a rocky ledge and stopped. They had reached the summit.

John had taken this route before, and now he pointed to a house far down the other side of the mountain. "See that farm? We can cook dinner there. But look—" He swept his arm to the horizon, and Isobel gazed at the blue and violet mountain peaks that stretched, range after range, into the distance. Lisu country?

"Yes!" John exclaimed. "Those are the mountains of the Salween Canyon where the Lisu live. We ought to be there by tomorrow night."

At dawn they were on their way again, Isobel feeling much stronger, and they followed a dusty winding trail that took them closer and closer to the Salween River. By evening they had reached Six Treasuries, a little market town on the bank of the Salween where three Chinese warlords lived. A feudal system still operated in these mountains. The Chinese warlords who owned the land acted as feudal masters and regarded the Lisu as mere animals, useful only to farm the land and pay taxes. "Monkey people," was their contemptuous name for the Lisu tribesmen whose villages perched high on the mountainsides. The warlords, immensely rich, had built castles complete with gun turrets, huge pillars, and hand-carved furniture.

One of the warlords had invited Isobel and John to supper, and he showed them through his glistening white castle, proudly pointing out its fortifications. But Isobel was far more impressed when John took her out to look across the Salween Canyon. Black mountain peaks jutted up against the starlit sky, and on their dark sides glimmered countless tiny lights.

"Fires?" whispered Isobel.

"Yes, Belle," said John. "Lisu fires. Those are Lisu villages over there."

"Oh, John!" A verse flashed into Isobel's mind. *My sheep wandered through all the mountains, and upon every high hill: yea, my flock was scattered upon all the face of the earth, and none did search or see after them. . . .* These are the Lord's other sheep, she thought, remembering, *Other sheep I have, which are not of this fold: them also I must bring.* Thank you, Lord, she prayed, for bringing us at last to these sheep of yours. Enable us to lead them into your fold.

By noon the next day they had reached a Lisu village—just a huddle of spindly bamboo shanties that clung to the mountainside. They stopped to eat with a Christian family, and Isobel was warmed by the friendliness of their smiles. She admired the embroidery on the women's blue skirts and the graceful manner in which they wore their navy blue turbans, and she wished she knew some Lisu so she could understand their cheerful comments.

But not all the villagers were Christians; she could tell that at a glance. She had heard much from J. O. Fraser about the Lisu's fear of demon "bites." He had described how they thought a demon might hide anywhere, even in trees and rocks, and how the people laid offerings of rice, incense, and red paper charms on their demon shelves in hopes of appeasing the angry demons. Many of the women's faces were dark and dull, and Isobel's heart went out to them immediately.

After lunch John took her to a ridge high above the Salween Canyon so they could look across at the mountains on the other side. He pointed out a trail that clung to the rocky slopes, winding back and forth until it disappeared over the top. "Just around that corner, in Pine Mountain Village," he said, "that's where Leila Cooke lives."

Isobel took a deep breath. Just around that corner? She glanced up at the encircling mountains, then down at the cliffs that dropped thousands of feet below them into snarling green water.

"Yes," said John. "You and I still have to go all the way down into the ravine, across the river, and up that trail before we get there."

By late afternoon they had climbed far enough up the trail to see three small brown huts in the distance. "One of those is Leila's house," John said. And just beyond would be Pine Mountain Village, Isobel thought. Was Leila Cooke at home? She caught sight of a red sweater. Yes, she must be; a Lisu wouldn't be wealthy enough to own one of those.

But now Isobel wanted to hang back. How would this woman feel about strangers just dropping in on her? Mrs. Cooke was well known for her devotion to the Lisu and for the books she had written about them. She was probably solemn and middle-aged, engrossed in her work, with no time for guests. John must have been thinking the same thing, for he gave Isobel a worried smile. "Now Belle, you know how you like to *talk*. Just remember who she is and try to restrain yourself."

"Yes, of course." The red sweater was moving closer and closer down the winding trail, and Isobel resolved to be as dignified as possible.

A few minutes later she was clasped in a loving embrace. "Oh, how good to see you," cried Leila Cooke. Chattering merrily, she led them the rest of the way to her shanty, which was spacious and clean, although it had only bamboo matting for walls and floor. An iron cooking stove and a little heater stood in the corner; at least it would be warm enough, Isobel thought.

Soon they were drinking hot tea and eating Leila's muffins while she explained how her husband had left a month before to help the young church up at Luda. She had been expecting Isobel and John to arrive any day.

That evening, Lisu young people crowded into the Cooke's home for their usual visit. Sometimes they studied Chinese, Leila explained, or learned a new Lisu hymn, or had a class in reading.

Isobel and John met Moses, the Lisu pastor, and during the next few days they helped Leila as much as they could in her ministry with the young Lisu church. Church leaders came from all over the district for the Sunday service, and Leila pointed them out. One, a tall young man with a bright, intelligent face caught Isobel's attention.

"That's Me-do-me-pa, the headman of Oak Flat Village," said Leila. "He's done some good preaching down south in the Village of Horse Grass Level. A few years ago he was beaten by the warlord for being a Christian, but he lived through it and the church is stronger than ever because of him." She smiled. "I call him 'The Shepherd' because he has such a heart of love and care for the rest of the flock."

One morning while they sat in Leila's hut, three handsome men wearing white clothes and red turbans walked in. They refused Leila's offer of chairs, and, squatting on the floor, began to talk earnestly to her in Lisu. Isobel watched them curiously. They must have come from some distance, since the Lisu in this area wore navy blue turbans.

Leila Cooke's dark eyes began to sparkle as she questioned the men. Every once in a while she made a quick translation into English so Isobel and John could keep up with the story. "This is Mark and his two friends; they've journeyed seven days from Goo-moo in Burma, far over the mountains—" Leila waved at the jagged white peaks visible through her open doorway. "They had to fight their way through the snow at the Great Pass—they came on behalf of their village to get teachers about Jesus—" She listened to them for another minute and then shook her head. "They heard about Him eleven years ago, but they have no books and no teachers; they're determined to stay until someone agrees to go back with them."

After a while the men from Goo-moo went off with Pastor Moses. "What an amazing story," exclaimed Leila. "How I wish we had a teacher to send with them! There's Simon, but he won't be back for a month." She smiled at Isobel and John. "I told them we didn't have a teacher right now and they said they would just wait. Meanwhile, they want to study with Pastor Moses."

Another Lisu Christian came in then and the day's work began, but Isobel had seen the gleam in John's eyes. She knew he would not forget about Mark and the men from Goo-moo.

A few days later, Leila left to go north and help her husband with the short term Bible school he wanted to have at Luda. Isobel and John kept up the work as well as they could, glad that a few of the Lisu Christians and Pastor Moses spoke Chinese. All too soon, their month-long visit passed. They had learned much about the Lisu work, but nothing had been settled yet about the opium persecution.

The Lisu Christians wanted John to stay until something was decided, but Isobel had promised the young missionaries at Yung-ping that she would return in a month. Finally they decided that John would stay and Isobel would make the trip back across the mountains escorted by Ma Fu-yin, a Christian who had traveled in with them. She would ride Jasper, the old mule J. O. Fraser had given them, and Lisu carriers would go along to help.

Chapter Nine

The long trip across the mountains gave Isobel plenty of time to think. From the broad, swaying back of her mule, she watched the miles slip by and considered what a move to Lisu country might mean to their future.

Conditions would be rough, since insects and dirt were just as much a problem in the Lisu's bamboo huts as they were in the hovels of the Chinese peasants. Living in the mountains would be even more primitive than living with the Chinese, for the Lisu did not even use furniture. They ate from a board on the floor, slept on a raised plank, and stored their grain in rough cupboards or baskets.

Supplying just the basics of food, water, and heat would take endless time and effort, Isobel could see. Leila had told her that servants were a necessity for the missionary who wanted to have time for preaching or teaching, although servants would be hard to find, because the Lisu were an independent people.

But up on those mountain slopes Isobel had felt stronger than she had on the hot plains of China, and it was sheer joy to see the magnificence of God's creation wherever she looked. Best of all were the Lisu Christians themselves: men like Me-do-me-pa and Pastor Moses and the teacher-evangelist Job—warm-hearted and earnest; and how they loved to sing! It would be a privilege to spend her life teaching such a people about the Lord.

John did not get back to Yungping until June, two months later, but as soon as he did, they wrote a letter to J. O. Fraser. They described the trip, explained what was happening in the Lisu work, and emphasized that Isobel felt strong enough to handle life in the mountains. His answer seemed long in coming, but it brought good news: they could move to Lisu country until time for their furlough, almost two years away.

Then, just as they began to make plans, John contracted amoebic dysentery. No sooner had he recovered than it became apparent that he needed hernia surgery, so Isobel took him to the new doctor at the CIM station in Tali. Weeks turned into months, and it was December before John was well enough to travel and they could start packing for their long trip.

Since their nearest source of supplies would be at least six days' journey away, Isobel tried to think of everything that she and John and especially Kathryn might need. Food, of course, particularly flour, sugar, and canned goods. Clothes too; furniture, books, tools; and plenty of kerosene for their lanterns. She couldn't forget her "baby organ" that the Corner Club girls had given her. And what about medicine? She'd better go prepared; sending a message to the nearest doctor would take two months.

It looked like a mountain of supplies, Isobel thought, but each item was necessary. Even the money they would use—heavy silver coins—had to be packed along with everything else. She and John filled box after box until finally the eleven pack mules were loaded and they could set off on their adventure.

They traveled back up the Mekong River valley, enjoying bright sunshine and cool weather. Before long they had left Chinese civilization behind. Now they journeyed through a wilderness of mountains strewn with rocky slopes and steep-walled canyons. For the first part of the trip, Isobel and Kathryn rode in sedan chairs carried by porters, and John rode Jasper, the mule. On the steepest slopes Isobel rode the mule and John walked, but Kathryn stayed in her sedan chair.

At night they slept in Chinese inns, and finally they reached the old farmhouse they had named "The Dirtiest Inn in the World." It was a challenge to keep any child clean in that sooty place, and by the time morning came, Isobel was glad to get Kathryn outside so she could give the little girl's hands one last wash. After they loaded the mules, John led in prayer, and they began the long steep climb that Isobel remembered well. At least she wasn't sick this time.

Up and up they followed the trail, through the bamboos, through the pine belt, into the ancient forest hung with creepers. At the top they halted to catch their breath, and Isobel gazed longingly across a sea of cloud-draped mountain peaks and shadowy canyons. Through one of those dark gorges flowed the Salween River, and by its side lived the Lisu people. . . .

Meanwhile, the trail plunged back down the other side of the mountain, and it would be hard traveling, especially for the mules. Down they went, skidding and sliding, down and further down, until the cliffs crowded them close to the bottom of the ravine. The mules fell behind, and they were still out of sight by nightfall, but they would catch up, John said.

Early the next morning, the small group started off on a level road that followed a chattering stream, but huge gray rocks hung threateningly over their heads. In some places the rocks had fallen and the travelers had to pick their way across wide landslides, but they pressed on through the wilderness. Near noon they came upon a few Chinese huts beside a sulphur spring; John managed to buy a piece of rock salt and wood for a fire so they could cook oatmeal for lunch.

By this time the mule train had caught up, and as Isobel and John were eating, their young muleteer hurried up to them. "You will have to go back—the mules will never make it," he exclaimed. "It was hard enough for them to climb the mountain yesterday, but these landslides are impossible!"

Isobel put a comforting arm around Kathryn and prayed as John tried to reason with the boy. They couldn't afford to turn back and take the other route—not after five days' journey—and they were running out of food, except for what was packed on the mules. The oatmeal they'd just eaten was their last. Besides, hadn't God led them to come this way?

Together she and John prayed the words that J. O. Fraser had taught them to use when obstacles to a straight path suddenly appeared. "Lord, if this be from Thee, we accept it; but if it is from Satan, we refuse it." Then they asked God to show them what to do.

As Isobel lifted her head, she saw the answer shining in John's eyes, and her heart echoed the same quiet word: *trust.* They would go forward and trust the Lord for His will concerning the pack mules.

"You must try it," John said to the muleteer. "Lighten the loads and make two trips across the landslides if you have to, but keep going. I think you can make it."

They forged on ahead of the mule train, and the landslides grew more and more dangerous. After each crossing, Isobel stopped and prayed for safety for each mule with its precious load. At the last landslide, they met travelers coming the other way who told them that the English consul had lost all his supplies at that very spot, just a week earlier. An English consul this far into the mountains? thought Isobel, and she forgot to pray over that particular landslide as they hurried on their way.

By nightfall they had reached the canyon of the Salween River—Lisu country—and Isobel's spirits rose. The next day at noon, John stopped the carriers at the Lisu village of Deer Pool. "There's a fine Christian girl named Homay in one of these huts, and we're going to have lunch with her," he told Isobel. "Be especially nice to her, Belle; she stands alone and needs comfort. She can speak a bit of Chinese too, so you two can talk together."

Isobel nodded, curious about this girl who had earned such praise from John. As she guided Kathryn past the pigsty and into the hut, a short, plump Lisu girl came running out. The girl called a greeting in Lisu, then politely switched to Chinese when Isobel did not answer. Isobel liked Homay right from the start—she seemed such a cheerful, tidy, capable girl. And she took good care of Kathryn, washing her bowl and carefully preparing her rice. As John had said, she was a remarkable person.

The next day a plump, blue-clad figure joined them at their noon stop, and Isobel looked at Homay in surprise. The girl carried a roll of bedding on her back. "Are you planning to come and stay with us?" Isobel asked. She had been praying about the matter of servants, but she hardly dared hope that this bright girl might consent to help them.

Homay smiled shyly, her face earnest under its dark blue turban. "Yes, if you want me to." As they talked, Isobel learned that Leila Cooke had suggested to Homay that she might want to cook for the new missionaries, and Homay, after thinking it over, had decided that it would be a good way to learn about God.

After a hearty lunch of rice, bacon, and eggs, the small group started on the last leg of their trip. They followed a yellow brown trail that spiraled further and further up the side of the mountain, and they reached the crest just as the sun was sinking out of sight.

Through the chilly twilight Isobel recognized a man coming down the trail toward them. Good, she thought, it was Job, the Lisu evangelist; what a relief that he could speak Chinese!

Job offered to go down the mountain and direct the coolies, and Isobel and John hurried on, the night darkening around them.

"Here we are," John said at last, and Isobel plodded toward a group of huts that clung to the hillside. She followed John into one of the shanties and stood there, shivering. The single room was bare, except for a few rough cupboards covered with dust. She reminded herself that the Cookes had moved up to Luda months ago; that was why everything looked so cold and empty. Little Kathryn glanced around. "Let's just stay here a couple of days and then go, huh?" She ran outside, and John went after her.

Alone, Isobel stared at the bamboo-mat walls wavering in the wind. There wasn't even any food here. She rubbed her icy hands together. And what about their own boxes of food—what if they had been lost? Her eyes filled with tears of fatigue. A dusty paper pinned to the wall caught her attention. It must have been left by the Cookes, she thought, stepping over to read the crayoned words: *My God shall supply all your need.*

The simple verse sent a warm flame of comfort into her heart. Forgive me, Lord, she cried silently. Forgive me for forgetting that *You* brought me here. She blinked away her tears and went to look for John. He and Kathryn were in a nearby hut, kneeling before the fire while their helpers prepared a supper donated by neighbors. They called out to her in welcome, and she joined them gratefully.

It wasn't until several days later that the pack mules arrived. Their muleteer reported that they had crossed each landslide safely except the last one. That's the crossing I forgot to pray for, Isobel thought with regret. The boy went on to explain that one of the mules had fallen over the edge of the trail into the river and some boxes of medicine had been lost, but the mule had survived.

Now that everything was here, Isobel set about the job of unpacking; at last she could make their little shanty a home. In her first letter after the move, she described it:

> Our Lisu house has only braided bamboo mats for a floor over the earth, so we live much like kittens in a basket. The roof is formed of wooden stakes laid on the beams and held down by logs. There are no nails used in the building, everything being tied together with bark.
>
> It's true, the walls are rather porous and, as a matter of necessity, the weather is a member of the family, coming and going out at will. One morning at breakfast, a little white cloud walked in our door! It vanished the next second—guess we scared it away! The clouds up here are a continual marvel of beauty.

Chapter Ten

Before Isobel could catch her breath, she and John were swept into the bustle of preparations for the Christmas festival. Christmas was the one time of year when Lisu Christians from all parts of the Salween Canyon came to gather around the missionaries. The host church in Pine Mountain Village erected temporary huts of pine boughs, set up dozens of simple cook stoves, and constructed an arch of greenery to welcome their guests.

The day before Christmas, a lookout was posted to watch the trails, and as soon as he saw the line of travelers that meant visitors, he fired a two-gun salute. While the gunshots were still echoing down the canyon, Christians ran to meet the newcomers, and the reception committee lined up under the arch, ready to sing their welcome song and shake hands.

The guests were heavily laden with bedding, weapons, and contributions of food, but each one was eager to shake hands. Ever since the days of J. O. Fraser's pioneering, hand-shaking had become a Christian sign.

The day after Christmas was set aside for the baptism of new Christians. As the twenty-nine candidates marched in procession over the hilltop, Isobel took Kathryn and climbed up onto a huge rock to watch. Among the deacons lined up on one side of the mountain pool, she recognized the tall form of Me-do-me-pa. Behind the deacons stood a volunteer choir singing "O Happy Day." On the other side of the pool waited the new believers, shivering in their thin garments as the December wind swept down from the heights of Pine Mountain.

After a quick plunge into the icy water, each believer shook hands all the way down the long line of deacons, then ran for shelter and dry clothes. The cold water and bitter wind made baptism an ordeal, and Isobel couldn't help comparing it with the comfortable baptisms she had seen at home. What a love for God these mountain Christians have, she thought. Thank you, Lord, for bringing me to work with them.

After Christmas, the church deacons decided that Isobel, Kathryn, and John should move to Oak Flat Village, since the Christians there were more deserving of a resident missionary. The Cookes, as senior missionaries, approved the change, and Isobel packed up their household things once more. Homay came too, for she was now a good friend and helper.

In January 1935, Isobel wrote to friends describing their new location:

> About three miles crawling up the southern trail, and still on the Pine Mountain range, the path comes to a kind of huge knoll, dotted with old gnarled oak trees. The rock cliffs, with here and there a lacy pine tree to add colour, lift abruptly above this high little tableland, and scrub-tree covered mountain sides sweep steeply down from its edge. Here is the village of Oak Flat where Me-do-me-pa, "The Shepherd," lives.

The sunny spring months of January, February, and March soon gave way to summer, the rainy season in Lisu country. The rain brought out the wild orchids that cascaded from dead old trees, but it turned the mountain paths to mud. In spite of the chilling drizzle, Isobel made many trips to the surrounding villages, sometimes with Kathryn and Homay. In July, at the height of the rainy season, she and John and Kathryn made a longer tour of several villages, but when Kathryn came down with malaria, they decided that such traveling was too dangerous for a white child. After that, Isobel and John took turns making short trips to nearby villages and John went on the long journeys by himself.

When it was Isobel's turn to go visiting, she was usually escorted by a Lisu teacher whom she named Lisu John to avoid confusion with Husband John. One dark morning when Lisu John arrived at her shanty, he said, "*Ma-ma* (Lady-teacher), why don't you stay home today? It is raining and snowing; the trail will be dangerous with landslides."

She gazed at him, standing there with his blue trousers rolled up to avoid the mud, straw sandals on his bare feet. "Are you staying home, John?"

"Of course not." He looked surprised.

"Well, I'm not staying home either." And they started off on an hour's climb up the slippery trail.

As they drew close to the village, Isobel wondered again how the Lisu shanties could keep from falling down the steep mountain slope. It must be the long wooden stilts, she decided. The stilts supported the front porch of each hut, keeping it level, and the space under the floor made a useful shelter for the cattle.

They entered a dark, smoky hut, and the hostess greeted them, hurrying to prepare hot tea. Isobel sat and rested, looking around herself with interest. She certainly could smell the animals under the house; in fact she could almost see them through the wide cracks at her feet. What was that pink thing down there on the floor? A piece of raw meat? But it was moving. She leaned forward to get a better look: oh, a cow's tongue! As the cow finished licking something off the slats, she sat back again.

Meanwhile, Lisu John had been studying his Gospel book, and soon he began to ask her questions. Since J. O. Fraser had not yet finished translating the whole Bible into Lisu, the Christians had only the Gospels and the Acts, but Lisu John never seemed to grow tired of discussing them.

Knowing the spiritual qualities of Lisu John, it was no surprise to Isobel when her husband chose him to go along on a trip to the Goo-moo people in Burma. Ever since young Mark and his companions had appeared at Leila Cooke's door to beg for help, Isobel and John had prayed for them. And this September the way had opened for John to go. It was seven days' journey one way, far to the west, so he would be gone for more than a month, but he left Job the evangelist with Isobel so she would have a Lisu interpreter.

No sooner had John disappeared into the mountains than Homay received a message that her father was dying. She had no choice but to go back to Deer Pool Village and take care of him.

Isobel missed her cheerful helper, and Kathryn kept asking when she'd come back, but they managed to get along until the morning Isobel awoke feeling ill and feverish. Strange red patches with blisters appeared on her face, and her fever went higher and higher. Just as Isobel had to take to her bed, Homay returned from her father's funeral, and what a joy it was to see that dear smiling face again!

While Isobel was sick, Homay took care of Kathryn, and the little girl was well fed, for she liked the Lisu foods—rice, corn, and pumpkins. But Isobel was too sick to eat. Each night the Lisu came to sing and to pray for her, and Job visited several times a day. He wanted to go to Paoshan for a nurse, but Isobel told him no, it would be two weeks before he got back, and surely she would be well by then. She tossed and turned on her wooden plank. I've got to get well, she thought. If Mr. Fraser hears of this, he'll say, "You've only been there for eight months, and see, you're sick already."

But Isobel's fever hung on; she could not eat the rough Lisu food, and she grew weaker each day. Homay tried hard to find some meat or some eggs, but this was a famine year and none were available. Finally Job got up one morning at 4:00 and set off for Paoshan, and Isobel was too weak to care. She felt so hot and dirty—if only she could have a bed-bath. Perhaps Homay could help?

Carefully she explained the procedure to Homay, who seemed to be quite mystified. But the anxious girl hurried off for a basin of hot water. She dipped her hands into it and spread the water across Isobel's feverish skin. No, that wasn't what Isobel meant, but it would have to do.

Meanwhile, Job had run his feet into blisters, making the six-day trip east to Paoshan in four days, but it was still two weeks before he could get back to Oak Flat Village. With him came two CIM nurses, and they brought a folding camp bed, medicines, and food.

They lifted Isobel from her sleeping boards onto the camp bed, and she felt as if she were floating on a cloud. Her illness was diagnosed as erysipelas, a skin disease. Even more worrisome, the nurses found that she had been slowly starving to death. Since nourishing food was so hard to get at that time of year, they decided to carry Isobel out to Paoshan. Homay went along too, so she could care for Kathryn and help Isobel continue learning the Lisu language.

In Paoshan Isobel slowly regained her strength and enjoyed spending some extra time with Kathryn. She also did some thinking about what had happened to her while John was away. God's watchful grace had kept them from many dangers, but there were things they could do to help themselves. The problem of getting proper food, for example, would not have arisen if they had taken time to plant a garden and raise chickens; then they would have been better prepared for the time of famine.

Three months later, after plenty of rest and good food had restored Isobel's health, J. O. Fraser gave permission for her to return to Oak Flat. She and Kathryn and Homay were just in time for the Christmas festival.

We had a wonderful welcome back to Oak Flat on December 16. Halfway down the mountain John met us, accompanied by Ye-chia-me (Kathryn's playmate), Gu-fu-chee (banging the chapel gong) and Mark. The rest of the crowd was ordered to be in ceremonial line farther up the hill, but on hearing our voices Plum Tree Flat-ers could not contain themselves and came pelting down on us, led by Caleb with his big boyish laugh and gripping handshake.

John had reported encouraging results from his visit to Goo-moo, and three or four Christians, including Mark, had made the long trip back to Oak Flat. Besides coming for the festival, the Goo-moo Christians wanted to talk to Isobel and John one last time before their furlough next year.

Isobel's favorite part of the Christmas festival was the testimonies. She and Kathryn settled themselves on the rough-hewn benches of the chapel and listened. Lisu Christians jumped to their feet two or three at a time to speak, and the piles of burning pine chips threw a flickering light on one earnest brown face after another. This is marvelous, Isobel thought.

One whom she especially noticed that Christmas was Joseph, a young man who had endured persecution from his own family for refusing to worship the demons. His sunny smile and soft dark eyes were often directed at Homay, and Isobel was amused to see that Homay did not seem to mind at all.

As part of their Christmas festivities, the Lisu also donated money to missionary work in other places. Poor though they were, they gladly cooperated in sending a gift to Amy Carmichael's work with children in faraway India.

To begin the new year of 1936, Isobel and John's big project was house building. Experienced missionaries told them that their small, leaky hut was not a healthy place to live and suggested that John build a better house. They would call it "House of Grace," Isobel and John decided, and it would be very simple, equipped with nothing more than necessities, so the Lisu would feel at home there too. No curtains, for example. The Lisu considered it a waste of precious cloth to put up curtains, and they could not understand why the foreigners would want to hide themselves away in such a manner.

The Lisu Christians helped get the house started, pitching in with their long knives to skin the bark off thirty pine trees cut up on Sunset Ridge. They used a large saw to square the logs, turning them into joists or beams. The log framework went up quickly, and before long the roof was in place. But even with all their efforts, the February rains swept down before they could finish the bamboo-mat walls.

Isobel had been hoping to get the house finished before the Cookes arrived, any day now, to help with a week of Bible teaching. She described those last frantic days with a flourish:

Lisu usually do not work in such weather, but the faithful little group agreed, and despite their thin garments, and the penetrating damp chill, they threw themselves into valiant effort, Homay cheering them on, occasionally with cups of hot tea or steaming honey water. And by Saturday night, the two rooms were walled and ready for occupation. Then, as we were in the midst of finishing touches, a cry came echoing over the knoll— "They're coming!" and John came running in upon me, "Belle! Cookes are here! Cookes are here! Just climbing the hill now!" The next moment we parted as if a bomb had burst us asunder—he to the right to welcome our guests, and I to the left to the bedroom to pull out dresser scarfs and linen that had been packed away from the building dust.

During the week of Bible school, Isobel found out how truly musical the Lisu Christians were. As J. O. Fraser had said, they delighted in learning new hymns and often memorized all four parts to sing in harmony. The little organ she had brought from America added a great deal of enjoyment to their songfests.

Whenever she had a chance, Isobel liked to slip out onto the trail that zigzagged through the trees to Sunset Ridge. There, perched on a favorite rock or hidden in a clump of pines, she could have her prayer time alone with the Lord. Like the Chinese, the Lisu thought her desire to be alone rather strange, but at least in Lisu country she could find some secluded places; privacy was impossible in the crowded villages and open plains of China.

After Bible school was over, the Cookes went back to Luda and John finished up the House of Grace. Isobel began to pack for their furlough with bittersweet anticipation. She needed the rest, but it would be difficult to leave these people; already they seemed a dear family—Moses, Job, Me-do-me-pa, Lisu John, and of course, Homay. But what would happen to Homay while they were gone? She made it a matter for serious prayer and wrote to her prayer partners about it, since Homay's heathen brothers, greedy for her dowry, were threatening to sell her to a heathen man as a wife or a slave.

To Isobel's relief, young Joseph suddenly overcame his shyness and sent Homay a proposal note. Everyone was astonished when her brothers agreed to the marriage, but Isobel recognized it as an answer to prayer.

Joseph had volunteered for a six-month evangelistic trip to Goo-moo in Burma; when he returned, he and Homay would be married. Meanwhile, a letter arrived from Leila Cooke, asking if Homay might work for them while the Kuhns were on furlough. Homay agreed happily, and Isobel knew she would be in good hands until her wedding day arrived.

Chapter Eleven

It was March 1936 when Isobel and John left on their furlough, and for a year and a half they enjoyed visiting each other's family and friends. Even so, Isobel's beloved Lisu were never far from her mind, and she delighted in receiving letters from Homay, Me-do-me-pa, and others. The Cookes wrote regularly, giving details about the young church. One day Leila Cooke sent them tragic news: young Joseph had drowned on his way back from the evangelistic trip to Burma.

Oh, not Joseph! thought Isobel. Poor Homay. How terrible to lose him just before their wedding! And what a loss to the church. Joseph, with his pure spirit and his radiant smile, had been one of the best teachers.

Mrs. Cooke's letter said that Homay had accepted the news quietly, and later, from a nearby hut, they had heard her softly singing, "Have Thine own way, Lord; have Thine own way."

Homay's next letter to Isobel was typically Lisu in its restraint. She did not mention her loss, but she gave other tidbits of news. Mr. Fraser had come to visit the Cookes, and she was happy about helping him finish translating the New Testament into Lisu.

By August 1937, Japan was at war with China, but Isobel and John were allowed to return since they worked in southwest China, far from the conflict. They brought with them a typewriter capable of typing Lisu script and dreams of starting a Bible school during the rainy season.

Kathryn, now six years old, returned to China also, and it was time for her to go to school. Isobel hated the prospect of sending her little girl anywhere. Perhaps she could bear it if Rynna went to the school at Kunming; it wasn't far away, and she could stay with her aunt and uncle, the Harrisons.

But when they reached Hong Kong, a telegram from headquarters destroyed her hopes: SEND KATHRYN TO CHEFOO WITH GRACE LIDDELL.

Isobel folded the telegram into a tight square. Kathryn was to go all the way to Chefoo for school?

But Chefoo is on the east coast of China, more than a thousand miles away, she thought. I might as well send Rynna to the other end of the world!

She tried to sort out her fears. Kathryn didn't seem to mind the change in plans, and it was good that she wouldn't have to travel alone—Miss Liddell would be a fine escort. The Chefoo school was better equipped and staffed than the one at Kunming—that was good too. Considering the war with Japan, Chefoo would probably be safer than Kunming.

None of her careful reasoning made it any easier to say good-bye to Kathryn, and for hours afterward, Isobel grieved with all the intensity of her mother's heart. She couldn't eat; she couldn't sleep. John shared in her anguish, and he patiently walked with her through the streets of Hong Kong until she collapsed from sheer exhaustion.

During the long train trip back to Kunming she tormented herself with questions. When would she ever see her little girl again? Who would share her whispered secrets? Who would tuck her into bed? Who would care if Rynna were lonely and cried herself to sleep at night?

Finally the Lord spoke to her about handling her grief. She could think about Him rather than about her sorrow. She could turn her attention to helping someone else, instead of spending herself on useless emotion.

She thought about Homay, who had lost her Joseph. In writing about Homay's experiences, she had referred to a passage in Matthew 7, and now her own paraphrase of verse 25 lingered in her mind: *The rains of disappointment descended, and the floods of sorrow came, and the winds of questioning blew, and beat upon that house; and it fell not, for it was founded upon a rock.*

Floods of sorrow, Isobel thought. Homay had to deal with great sorrow. It was Christ who steadied her, and He's my Rock too; I have to focus my mind on Him alone.

Comforted, she was able to enjoy the grandeur of the mountains as the train climbed higher and higher toward Kunming, 6,000 feet above sea level.

In Kunming, a new disappointment awaited Isobel and John. The Mission had not reassigned them to the Lisu. J. O. Fraser wanted John to be his assistant superintendent for all of western Yunnan Province, and they were to be stationed at Paoshan.

John did not mind the new assignment since he enjoyed preaching to the Chinese, but Isobel felt as if another child had been torn from her arms. Not work with the Lisu? How could she bear it, not to go back? And Bible teaching was what she did best, not pioneer evangelism. At Paoshan there were only a few young converts to be taught, far different from the hundreds of eager Lisu who needed to learn the Word of God.

Fresh from the lesson God had taught her about sorrow, she took the whole situation directly to Him. She had made a habit of fasting and praying one morning each month, and now she decided to spend the day of October 1, 1937, in special prayer for the Lisu at Oak Flat Village. At the same time she asked the Lord to deal with her longing to return.

He reassured her with a promise from the end of Zephaniah, chapter 3: *The Lord thy God in the midst of thee is mighty. . . . At that time will I bring you again . . . when I turn back your captivity before your eyes.*

Confident that the Lord would someday take her back into Lisu work, she packed happily for Paoshan, not telling even John about the verses God had given her. Less than two months later, they were on their way into Lisu country. J. O. Fraser called it a "temporary designation," since a situation had arisen in Oak Flat Village that required the help of missionaries who could speak Lisu. But Isobel knew that somehow God would work it out for them to stay.

At Oak Flat, the rejoicing Lisu met them under a welcome arch decked with flowers. Homay's shy smile was as bright as ever, and many friends asked about Kathryn. Me-do-me-pa threw his arms around John's neck and wept silently. During the long months of their absence he had taken an unpopular stand for what was right, and he had suffered for it.

The problems in the Lisu church strengthened John's conviction that their leaders needed an intensive period of Bible study. Now that the whole New Testament had been translated into Lisu, they needed to learn the teachings in Galatians and I Corinthians on law and grace. But when could those hard-working farmers take time off for Bible study? John had already decided that the rainy season might be best: it was a perilous time for white men to travel, and work on the farms was less urgent.

J. O. Fraser gave his approval for the project, and by the end of January 1938, the Mission had sent two young men to help with the work. Again and again Isobel whispered, "Thank you, Lord," as she saw their temporary designation stretch from a few weeks into several weeks and then into months.

Easter drew near, the first Easter they would spend without Kathryn. Her little girl was always on Isobel's heart; she prayed that the Lord would give Rynna an especially happy Easter and that she wouldn't be homesick, even though she was so far away.

For the young Lisu church, Isobel thought of a way to emphasize the importance of the resurrection. Job had told her how he and La-ma-wu, another Lisu Christian, had been the first to preach the gospel to the villages of the Upper Salween Canyon, almost ten years before. As the two young men neared Oak Flat on their way home, La-ma-wu had fallen sick and died from the Canyon's dreaded virulent fever.

Job had buried him by the roadside and then trudged home to tell the waiting wife and child how the young evangelist, only twenty-three years old, had given up his life.

"Has there never been any monument put up?" asked Isobel. Already she was beginning to make plans.

When Job explained that there wasn't even a well-marked grave and only he knew where to find it, Isobel declared, "The Lisu church ought never to forget La-ma-wu! And it will be grand and fitting that their first Easter service should be held at his grave."

Just before dawn on Easter morning, Isobel, Job and his wife, and another Christian girl stood on a jutting rock near the village of Border Mountain to awaken the village by singing "Christ the Lord Is Risen Today" and "I Know That My Redeemer Liveth." As they sang, sunrise crept over the eastern ridge of the canyon, pushing back the shadows and lighting the rocky mountain slopes. Ten other Lisu Christians slipped out of their huts to join them for a time of prayer and worship.

After breakfast, they held a regular Easter service, and to this larger group Isobel explained their desire to honor La-ma-wu and build him a proper grave. The Lisu Christians followed Job up the canyon, single file as usual, until he stopped at the right place, high on the mountainside.

The grave had almost disappeared under wild grass, but with everyone helping, they soon had it covered with a mound of rocks, Chinese fashion. The women had picked wild rhododendron on the way, and now they arranged a cross of red flowers over the mound and edged it with fragrant white blooms.

Job preached the message, since he had been La-ma-wu's comrade, and when he finished, they sang the Lisu funeral hymn, "Sleep On, Beloved." As the strains of the song drifted out over the rocky canyon, Isobel thought about the young life given and the hundreds of Lisu souls that had been saved. May I be faithful as well, she prayed—faithful to teach Thy Word to these, Thy beloved scattered sheep.

The weeks after Easter were filled with preparations for the three-month Rainy Season Bible School coming up in June. Isobel wanted to use some of the newly translated Bible books even though they were not yet printed, so Homay worked every day at the Lisu script typewriter to make copies for the students to study. The school would be mainly for Lisu evangelists, but church leaders were encouraged to come too.

John had good reasons for pursuing this project. The young evangelists had plenty of enthusiasm, and they knew enough Scripture to preach the good news of salvation, but Lisu converts up and down the canyon needed solid teaching in order to grow as Christians, and it was impossible for Isobel and John to reach them all.

Even with two other missionaries, there was no way they could teach in the dozens of widely scattered churches, some of them six days' journey away. Each Lisu evangelist could teach in several villages, multiplying the outreach. Besides, as J. O. Fraser had pointed out, it was better for the Lisu nationals to teach each other and build up a strong native church, independent of white missionaries.

John felt that it was important for the local church to have a part in supporting the evangelist-students, too. The young men had already made a considerable sacrifice by leaving their families and their farms, and they would have the expenses and dangers of traveling during the rainy season. John suggested to the church at Oak Flat Village that they should supply the students with food during RSBS.

The deacons, even Me-do-me-pa, were worried. "Food for fifteen for three months takes a lot of corn! It's never been done before. Where can the church find so much?" Me-do-me-pa asked. But John urged the deacons to trust God for a supply of corn, and they agreed to do it.

Chapter Twelve

The opening day of Rainy Season Bible School came at last. From villages all along the canyon, barefoot, roughly clad students climbed up to Oak Flat. They hung book bags over their shoulders and carried food and bedding on their backs.

On weekdays they met in a long weather-beaten bamboo shanty for courses in Bible study, personal evangelism, and preaching. They especially seemed to enjoy learning new hymns and singing them in four parts, accompanied by Isobel on the little organ. On weekends, despite the constant rain, they went out by pairs to the surrounding villages, some as far as twenty-five miles away, to preach at the Sunday services.

Isobel observed each student with interest and wrote long letters about them to her prayer partners. Lucius was tall and handsome, with curly black hair and a joyous smile. His enthusiasm and hard work had already earned him a job as the Kuhns' helper.

Twenty years old, [he] comes from Village-of-the-Olives, the only child of Christian parents and supported by them in these study groups. . . . He is quick as a flash, sits next to the bottom of the class, but leads it. John says, "He stretches his long neck around the corner of the table—and misses nothing." Quick of mind, his thoughts outrace his tongue so that his words often come forth on the stampede. Has the shyness and high-strung mettle of a thoroughbred colt.

Another of Isobel's favorite students was Job the evangelist:

Thirty-two years old, [Job] comes from Stockade Hill district, has believed for eighteen years; is the man who first brought the gospel to these parts. Small, slight, pockmarked, undignified; with his hat often stuck on a side corner of his head [he] looks more like a horse jockey than an evangelist. Perhaps the most insignificant-looking member of the class, but as far as we know, the greatest soul-winner Lisuland has yet produced. Job has so few natural gifts, and yet has been so used of God, that he is a monument of what God can do with any man who brings Him nothing much more than a heart of purposeful devotion.

"Purposeful devotion" could well describe each of the students, Isobel thought. In spite of their differing abilities—some could not yet read—each one wanted to learn and to be used of God. Sometimes, when she walked over to her prayer spot on Sunset Ridge, she passed one or two students who had gone out on the mountainside to pray too.

A few girls came to Rainy Season Bible School, including Homay, who had an advantage over the others since she had typed out Galatians and I Corinthians for the students to study. Isobel had found that if each student read along in his own copy, he could more easily understand the new words and concepts she was trying to teach.

The Lisu language had a wide vocabulary for different kinds of sin; for example, it had several words for describing how to skin a human being alive. But it had no word for "holiness" or for "conscience" or for "humility," so those words had to be invented by the missionary-translator and then carefully taught. Although the Lisu did have a word for God, *Wu-sa,* they did not worship Him; all their energies seemed to be spent on appeasing the demons.

For Homay, this Rainy Season Bible School was particularly eventful. One of the evangelist-students, Thomas, had been courting her for some time, and finally, at the end of the school session, they were married. Isobel was keenly interested in her good friend's wedding.

She is the best to be had in Lisuland, as Thomas well knew, and Homay was conscious that she could not say yes to a more faithful or finer Christian, so I think that was how it happened; but happiness seems to increase in their hearts every day. Homay was dressed in a combination of orange silk and dark blue cotton. . . . I played Lohengrin's "Bridal March" as they entered and left the chapel, and the whole ceremony was holy and quiet—a memory. Thomas is to be kept in this district for a while at least, and they live in a little house right next to ours, for Homay continues to help us in typing and in the house work.

By the end of Bible school, the deacons who had decided to trust God for enough corn saw a tangible reward for their faith. The students' weekend ministries were such a blessing to the surrounding villages that gifts came pouring in to the Oak Flat church. The gifts were more than enough to pay for the extra corn, and the thankful deacons voted to hold Rainy Season Bible School each summer after that.

Less promising than the eager Bible school students was Isobel's new goatherd. She first met the boy one evening when John was away, and she had invited him to share the meal with her and Homay:

I beheld a little fellow (looked like nine years old, but they said he was seventeen) seated on his haunches, with his head lowered and staring at me with the glare of a little wild animal. I did not feel comfortable.

Trying to make him feel part of the group, Isobel asked him to pray, but he growled a refusal, and she ended up asking the blessing herself. "Is he a Christian?" she asked Homay later. "Where did we ever get him?"

"Yes, he's a believer, but he isn't baptized yet," Homay said. "His mother is blind and a widow, and he is her only son."

Isobel nodded. The church had probably hired him for the sake of his blind mother, since the boy's wages would keep her from starving. Even so, many times during the next weeks and months Isobel wanted to get rid of him. Not only was he careless, he was full of his own importance; he snapped a haughty retort if she asked why the goats gave a quart of milk one day and only a cupful the next. He's cheeky as a chipmunk, she decided, and from then on she thought of him as Chipmunk.

When the rainy season had passed and travel was more practical, Isobel and John decided to make the long journey to Goo-moo, the faraway village in Burma where John had preached before they left on furlough. Since then, Lisu teachers had made several trips to Goo-moo, but Isobel and John wanted to see for themselves how the young church was doing.

Everything was almost packed, one bright autumn morning, when they heard Lisu runners pounding up the trail. Isobel dropped the quilt she was folding and ran to the door. They must be bringing news, she thought. Terrible news, from the look on their faces. Had something happened to Kathryn?

Too soon she found out: J. O. Fraser was dead. He had come down with malignant cerebral malaria, and the necessary medicine had not been available. The Chinese doctors were able to do nothing for him.

The sunny morning darkened around her, and the mountain peaks blurred. She reached for John, hardly able to stand. Mr. Fraser—*dead?* Her friend; her adviser; her spiritual father; the one who had first told her about the Lisu . . .

Her mind veered away from her own pain. His wife—what must she be feeling? Isobel stumbled to her desk and began a letter for Roxie Fraser.

The very thought of you makes my hand tremble so and tears come so that I do not know how I can write. The Lisu have just walked in with their unbelievable message. . . . Times like this are when we just have to bare our face to the tempest and go on without seeing clearly, without understanding, without anything but naked faith.

The Lisu of Oak Flat district, poor though they were, collected twenty dollars in silver to pay for the cost of digging J. O. Fraser's grave. Even before the funeral, Lisu Christians traveled to Paoshan from all over the Salween Canyon. They came as representatives of thousands of believers scattered across the mountains, and they held a memorial service in which the prayers, hymns, and tributes were all in Lisu.

Isobel and John were acutely conscious of their loss:

There was no one else on earth who had such a complete knowledge of the details of our problems and so no one who could share so perfectly in our joys and sorrows. And he never disappointed us in that sharing. . . . John and I have, perforce, to enter an entirely new epoch of our lives, for life can never again be quite the same without him. But life does not stop for heartache. . . .

And even while they grieved, they had to go ahead with their plans for the trip to Goo-moo. Homay and Thomas would come along too, and Lucius, as well as three Christian Lisu, the cook, the mule boy, and three carriers. They still desperately needed an interpreter and guide through the wild Kachin country, and at the last minute, two Christian men joined them who were fully qualified.

After the first long day of travel, down into the canyon and up again, they camped for the night on a mountain ridge from which they could still see the roof of their house. But the second day took them up into a thick forest that Isobel called "dark overhanging shut-you-in forest." Through it they climbed upward eleven thousand feet to the wind-whipped bare rocks of the great Pien-Ma Pass.

By late afternoon they reached the Pass, and Isobel stopped to gaze at a breathtaking panorama. Behind her was China: range after range of snowclad mountains rolling into the distance. Before her was Burma: an endless vista of towering peaks dyed crimson in the setting sun. And far, far below waited the British border fort of Pien-Ma with its neat rows of soldiers' barracks.

They hurried down the mountainside in hopes of reaching the fort by dusk; but they found it deserted and decided to set up camp in the middle of the road. For the next three days they traveled through canyons hung with orchids and waterfalls, and once, passing high wooded cliffs, they heard unseen monkeys cry warnings to each other. At night Isobel made good use of her guitar when they sang and preached in tribal villages.

The discomforts of jungle travel were made worse by the inevitable leeches.

Underfoot, the little black wrigglers were legion. They stood on the dead leaves of the path, standing upright on their tails and waving back and forth in the air, for a foot to attack, hang on to, and suck. The mules' legs were blood-streaked that day and our dear barefoot band suffered equally.

The last day, they pushed on through the hot sun and leeches, only to be delayed for hours at the river that separated them from Goo-moo. The only way to cross it was by means of a flimsy two-passenger bamboo raft tied together with bark. The mules and horses did not want to cross at all; they turned back as soon as they felt the swift current. Darkness fell when half their party was on one bank and half on the other, and the raft rowers feared the unseen rocks, so they waited for the moon to rise.

Finally, by dim moonlight the animals arrived: tied to the raft by tail and one man holding their head, they had been made to swim for it.

We had no food with us and had eaten nothing since lunch. Goo-moo was still two thousand feet above our heads and that climb before us which is too steep to ride and where the traveler must go up holding on to the mule's tail. A drink of coffee all around and then we began. The trail was through dense vegetation twice our height—I could see nothing beneath my waist; my hands holding onto Jasper's tail were all that was within vision, except for a silver-laced gleam overhead where the moon was trying to penetrate the tropical canopy

*over us. I could not see where my feet were tread-
ing—we had seen big snakes that day and I
thought of the leeches, but I was reminded that
Christians walk by faith, and, throwing my cares
on Him in all that stiff climb, I stepped on nothing
to alarm me.*

By moonlight, then, but still sweltering in the heat, they climbed the last steep ridge, arriving at midnight. They met with a rousing welcome, first from Mark and then from the Christians lining the road.

The next weeks were filled with Bible teaching and plenty of singing and preaching to the tribespeople who crowded into the little whitewashed chapel. The villagers had built Isobel and John a bamboo hut, roofed with long, curly banana tree leaves, and Isobel was glad for the privacy it afforded at the end of a long day. But all too soon their visit had to end.

The Goo-moo Christians had become so fond of Homay and Thomas that they begged to have the young couple stay for six months more of Bible teaching. Isobel and John agreed to the plan, gave Homay and Thomas their leafy bamboo hut, and reluctantly took their leave.

*Parting was, as usual, mournful. The Goo-moo
Christians wept so that as we dropped down the
mountainside from them, it sounded like the wail-
ing for the dead, and I was relieved when they
finally changed it to calling to us like monkeys,
after we were too far beneath them to communicate
otherwise.*

Chapter Thirteen

It was hard to leave the Christians at Goo-moo, but Isobel was glad to get back to their own little House of Grace and the work at Oak Flat Village. December brought the Christmas festival; then it was a new year, 1939, and time to prepare for the next Rainy Season Bible School.

One Sunday while Isobel was giving out medicines and ointments as usual after the noon service, she noticed that Luke, one of the Christian men, stood waiting for her. Beside him slouched a teen-age Lisu boy who was notable for his sullen face and bristly black hair. Certainly not an attractive prospect, she thought as she turned to them.

"This fellow wants to confess his sin," announced Luke. He motioned to the young man. "Now go ahead."

"I have sinned against you," the boy muttered. "The second Christmas you were here, I came to the festival to see what it was like. But I wasn't born again then, and . . . I saw a pretty bag hanging on your wall and I stole it. I want to be a Christian now, a born again one, and I wronged you in something else too."

He shuffled his feet and lowered his voice. "I got some medicine from you once, and instead of returning the bottle to you I sold it, and kept the money. Here is the price of it, and I will pay you for the bag when I can get the money, later on." With an expression of abject shame, he put a silver half dollar in Isobel's hand.

She accepted his apology gravely and tried to encourage him to study God's Word. Then she asked Luke to talk further with him. A few weeks later she was happy to hear that the boy, now named Gad, had offered to go along on a preaching trip with Jonah, a Lisu evangelist. Gad had declared that he would carry Jonah's baggage if only Jonah would teach him to read and write. What a change of heart for a thief, Isobel thought.

Gad's attitude was a welcome contrast to the goatherd, Chipmunk. Eighteen years old, and that Chipmunk still can't read, Isobel thought. I've got to do something about him. One evening she called him in and tried to interest him in her plans. "If you could read, you'd be able to study God's Word for yourself—that's a good thing. Wouldn't you like to learn?"

He just stood there, blinking at her. "Come now, it's not that hard." Isobel tried to sound encouraging. "I'll help you. We can work on it every evening and before you know it—"

He did not protest, so she started the reading lessons. The next night he didn't show up, but he came when she sent for him. Night after night it was the same. He came when she called; he sat, and he listened. But he did not exert himself, and he didn't seem to be learning a thing. Sometimes Isobel wondered if she was wasting those precious evening hours.

That summer when the students came trooping in for Rainy Season Bible School, Gad came too. At least *he* wants to learn, Isobel thought, still discouraged from her sessions with Chipmunk. She did not have much hope for Gad as a scholar, but in a letter to her friends she asked for prayer on his behalf.

He sits . . . face lowered, looking up at you with such a black scowl you would think he was planning your murder. This is just poor Gad trying to concentrate . . . such an unattractive surface, a

*slow working mind behind it, but, we trust, a sin-
cere desire to do what is expected of him. I hope
some of you take a liking to Gad—a prayer liking.*

Isobel did notice, though, that each day after the students ran
out to the athletic field, Gad still sat in front of the blackboard,
slowly copying out the Bible notes he needed. And Gad was more
than willing to volunteer for the longest, most difficult preaching
trips. It seemed to Isobel that each time he went out, he returned a
little more confident and stronger in the Lord.

This year the Lisu Christians had constructed a new schoolhouse for Rainy Season Bible School—the first Bible school building they'd ever built. Large enough to seat thirty students, it had
bamboo mats for walls and roof and an earthen floor. Last year they
had all been crowded into one small church room, and Isobel
thought this was a big improvement.

*It has no need of windows, for [the] mats do not
reach the roof, and it possesses no door—everything nice and airy. The "desks" are crude slabs of
rough wood held up by tree boughs driven into the
earth, so they don't wobble! I love it.*

The weeks of RSBS from June to August were happy ones: the
students seemed more eager and cooperative than last year, and all
the weekend preaching trips were accomplished safely in spite of
wild, rainy weather.

The month of August brought a few sunny days that year. On
those rare occasions, the whole school family hiked to Sunset Ridge
for a picnic supper. There they set up the black pots that held their
supper of boiled corn and chunks of boiled pork, and they perched
around the fire on rugs or piles of leaves. Isobel sat on her rug in
the midst of the students, enjoying the cheerful chatter and watching
the pink and golden sunset flame across the sky. When twilight fell,
everyone joined in singing their favorite hymns.

At the end of RSBS came Closing Day. The students elected two valedictory speakers and a song leader for the program of music, speeches, and awards for work well done. Each student prepared a five-minute testimony and dressed in his best clothes, including a flower in his buttonhole. While Isobel played a march on the organ, they filed into the chapel with measured steps. Family members came from miles around to enjoy the ceremony, then they went home to tell neighbors and friends about the marvels of Rainy Season Bible School.

But near the end of the summer, a shadow fell across Isobel's happiness. Me-do-me-pa, headman and beloved deacon at Oak Flat, was obviously sick. They had sent him to a Chinese doctor at Paoshan, but no treatment seemed to help him; after several months it seemed that his disease was probably an incurable cancer.

Homay's husband, Thomas, had fallen ill too. All during RSBS he had suffered from severe headaches and pain around his eyes; he seemed to be going blind. Although he managed to struggle through the classes, by the end of RSBS, the missionaries knew he would have to get some expert medical help.

Finally they decided that Thomas should go to a mission hospital in Burma where he could get free treatment. It meant a long and expensive journey, and Homay, usually so calm and sunny-spirited, was much distressed. Isobel sympathized with her, for she knew that Homay was expecting their first child. Wishing she could do something more to help, Isobel put an arm around the plump little shoulders and said, "Don't worry, dear. God is faithful, and remember you are a daughter to us. You and Thomas will always have a place in our home."

After the rainy season was over, Isobel and John did a great deal of traveling up and down the canyon. That year the Cookes were away on furlough, and they had asked the Kuhns to keep an eye on their Lisu congregation at Luda. Job the evangelist was working there, and before long he wrote that Three Clans Village had a serious problem with quarreling.

"I think we'd better go up there and see what's happening," John said to Isobel. "Those quarreling Christians are going to be a bad testimony all over Luda."

"That's true," said Isobel. "But Mr. Fraser called that trail up the canyon the worst in all China. I don't think I can walk it."

John thought for a minute. "We could use the mules—our Jasper and Jessie can handle it."

Isobel nodded in agreement, and John said, "Maybe Luke and Lucius could go as evangelists, and we'll take some good deacons."

Isobel was reluctant to leave Homay, whose baby was due in a few weeks, and she knew Chipmunk wouldn't work on his reading while she was away, but it seemed imperative to make this trip. Cath and Victor Christianson, who had been working with them for a while now, could take over the responsibilities at Oak Flat. Maybe God would give them a time of blessing at Luda.

They left on a sunny November morning, and for six days they climbed the tortuous river road that wound north through the canyon. They were still following the river when a group from Three Clans Village came down the mountain to meet them, waving and shouting in welcome.

Farther on down the trail, they met another well-wisher who gave them an invitation to supper, then a wealthy farmer who offered them cold honey-water from his tea kettle. Not far behind came another group of villagers who urged Isobel to drink their hot honey-water.

They crossed the river on rafts and found hot tea waiting for them on the other side, then climbed the steep ascent to the village. At the top of the hill stood a welcome arch of wild orchids, with hundreds of Lisu waiting behind it. What a reception, Isobel thought. The crowds of smiling faces reminded her of John's comment that Three Clans Village was like the New York of Lisu country. She smiled back at them as she dismounted stiffly from her mule. After all the prayer and planning and the long, dangerous journey, it looked as though they were off to a good start.

Too soon, they learned that the smiling reception committees were actually representatives from the three quarreling clans of the village, each trying to outdo the others and gain the missionaries' favor. The three clans had been arguing for months about who owned the rights to the valuable wormwood trees in their mountain fields, and they hoped that John would settle it by deciding in favor of one clan or the other.

It was a complicated problem, and John met with the clan leaders for many long discussions. Since no one would give in, the most outspoken clan members began to talk about taking the matter to the Chinese magistrate. John pointed out that it would be dishonoring to Christ's name for quarreling Christians to take their problems to a heathen judge. He urged them to accept the church's recommendation, which asked them to be generous and forgiving to each other, even if they did not make as much of a profit as they wanted.

No, they did not want to do that, the clan leaders told John respectfully. They had decided to go ahead and ask the Chinese magistrate to rule on their disagreement.

The Chinese official came to inspect the disputed fields. They had to carry him on their shoulders free of charge, kill a pig and feed him royally, and then he went back home and sent them this word: "First tax—for weariness of feet"—the trouble of inspection, but the title amuses me, for his precious feet never touched the ground, so to speak—"$220.00; after this is paid me I will give judgment," which means the tax for that, and the tax for writing out the document, and other incidental charges will be made later after he received the Weariness-of-Feet Tax! Result—the

*quarrelers are sitting around holding their head-
aches and groaning.*

While the quarreling families groaned, Isobel and John wrote
letters to their prayer partners about the urgent spiritual situation in
Three Clans Village. They had learned from experience that prayer
was the only way to battle the evil powers that seemed to control
the villagers. Then they turned their attention to the other villages
in the district. They had planned to visit for only three weeks, but
the need was so pressing that John decided it might be better for
them to stay three months and do as much teaching as they could.

The change in plans meant that they would spend Christmas
there too, but Isobel did not let herself hope for gifts or any kind of '
American celebration. China was still at war with Japan, and the
Chinese post office had ruled that parcels containing certain forbidden items would not be allowed to enter the country. She knew from
past occasions that the usual gifts from America would be confis-
cated, since the list of forbidden imports included most things a
missionary would need.

Kathryn was still in school at Chefoo, and of course there was
no way they could visit her for Christmas. Even one of those
much-looked-for letters from Rynna was unlikely, since no one at
the school knew they were spending Christmas at Luda. This would
have to be a completely Lisu Christmas, Isobel and John decided,
but they could make sure it was a happy one for their people.

Early in December, they heard a tantalizing piece of news. Mr.
Morrison, working north of them with another mission, had received printed copies of the Lisu New Testament. Could this be
true? They had watched J. O. Fraser laboriously complete the
translation and had waited months for it to be checked and printed.
Was it really published?

Mr. Morrison must have known about their work in Luda, for
he wrote, asking for some of their Lisu hymnbooks, and John asked
if he could spare any New Testaments in return. He sent the few

copies he had left, and their arrival was a momentous occasion for Isobel and John.

Oh, the joy of owning a copy—it has not left me yet! I felt as I turned its pages that God had given me all the Christmas gift I needed to make me happy.

But on the evening of Christmas day, carriers from Oak Flat Village arrived. They brought mail that included a gift from Kathryn—a new photo of herself—and two packages from America that had somehow slipped across the border. They found candy in one of the packages and celebrated an American Christmas after all. "Isn't God amazing?" Isobel exclaimed. "He's the only one who could have timed our packages to arrive so perfectly!"

After Christmas, Job and Luke and the two deacons had to leave for their homes in the south, and as Isobel watched them go, her throat ached with unshed tears. Their little group had arrived with such hope for Three Clans Village. Surely good preaching and teaching would triumph over selfishness! And now Job and Luke, their two best evangelists were leaving, and in spite of all the hard work, the villagers were still as bitterly opposed to each other as ever.

But there's one good thing, she told herself. They're taking our letters to America and England with them. We shall see what the Lord will do.

Chapter Fourteen

Just a few days later, Isobel and John were cheered by the unexpected arrival of three Lisu men who had left their families and come to help until March. The new year of 1940 began with trips to the villages perched on knobby outcroppings scattered all over the mountain. The weather was good—"golden winter days" Isobel called them—but the rocky slopes were alarming. In one place the terrain was so steep that they had to climb the thirty-foot cliff by means of a notched-sapling ladder, leaving the unharnessed mules to scramble through dense brush and find their own way up the mountain.

In February, a shipment of Lisu New Testaments arrived, enough for everyone, and John declared that now they could have a February Bible school. He challenged Three Clans Village to be especially generous, asking each family to feed one or two students for the entire month, and most of them agreed wholeheartedly.

Their response made Isobel feel that the villagers really did want to do right, but they were in bondage to their clan traditions. The law of the clan decreed that whenever a clan member got into trouble, the whole clan had to back him up, even if he was guilty. Any man who did not comply would be disowned. In the case of the quarreling clans, a person who wanted to settle the argument with forgiveness would be breaking the law of the clan.

Bible school went on as planned, and blessings poured out in spite of the threat of a typhus epidemic. Isobel and John met the rumor of typhus with an intensive session of prayer, since it seemed to be an attempt by Satan to frighten the students into going home. Not one student left, and God continued to bless.

No sooner was Bible school over than more squabbling broke out in the church of Three Clans Village. Isobel and John listened to them and tried not to show their heartbreak. Had all their work been for nothing? But the last two days of their visit, an inexplicable change seemed to come over the village—the clan leaders' hearts seemed softer, more open to God's Word. John decided to take advantage of it.

The night before they left, he held a service in the chapel and gave the clan members a bold challenge: break free from the law of the clan. He held up two sets of paper arrows that he had cut out. On one set was written, I HAVE NO DESIRE TO PRACTICE THE LAW OF THE CLAN. On the other was written, I DESIRE TO PRACTICE THE LAW OF LOVE. Quietly John told them that Satan was using the law of the clan to keep them from following God. As Christians, the law of love in Christ should be what bound them close together.

Isobel found that her hands were shaking as John held up an arrow. "Each of you who wants to break free from the law of the clan, come here and take this clan arrow and burn it in the fire. Then I will give you a love arrow and you can keep it always." Isobel, trying to pray, was hardly able to breathe. One by one, the clan leaders walked up to John and took their arrows. They all came, except one powerful old man who sat with his head down, as still as a stone.

Meanwhile, bitter enemies asked forgiveness of each other. Isobel watched with awe as two brothers who had hated each other for twenty-six years were reconciled and shook hands in front of the whole group. Then John confronted the old man. "Are you going to be the only one in the village to refuse the law of love?"

Still he did not move.

Isobel wanted to get up and shake the stubbornness out of him. One unyielded heart would affect all the others. "Pray," she whispered to the woman next to her. "Pray for him!"

John was just about to close the meeting when the old man lunged to his feet. He shuffled to the front. John handed him a clan arrow and he thrust it into the fire; then, clutching the arrow of love, he made a sincere public apology to his most hated enemy. Through tears of joy, Isobel marveled as the two enemies shook hands.

That evening while she was writing in her diary, she stopped for a minute and looked over at John. "What an amazing thing it was to see God work in those hearts tonight! I don't think I'll forget it as long as I live." Later, she wrote:

I myself have never been present at such a scene as God gave us to see that night. . . . It was wonderful. Only God could have done it, and only God can maintain it, but He has decreed that you and I must help Him by . . . the travail of intercession.

Back in Oak Flat Village once more, Isobel was soon caught up in the lives of her Lisu family. Victor Christianson had worked wonders in teaching her goatherd, Chipmunk, whom he had named Amos. He could read! Perhaps not so surprising, though, when she thought about it. Last summer Victor had tenderly nursed the boy through typhus fever, and apparently Chipmunk had not forgotten. The boy had a fine tenor voice too, Victor had discovered. *I must remember to call him "Amos" from now on,* Isobel thought. *Maybe he won't be so much of a chipmunk anymore.*

Homay's little son was already several months old, and Isobel couldn't wait to see him. He was a good-sized baby with beautiful dark eyes, but he still cried a lot and Homay seemed to be exhausted all the time. When Thomas returned from the hospital completely cured, Isobel was sure that Homay would soon feel better.

Meanwhile, she had to train new servants to replace Homay and their other helper, both clever and industrious girls who now had to care for their own families. Joe, only nineteen, with a pimply face, unruly black hair, and a dignified manner, was her new cook. He had much to learn, but at least he tried to please. The new girl who was supposed to be his helper turned out to be less than satisfactory.

Training the two of them was a trial that Isobel dreaded, but she persisted, managing to keep her sense of humor at the same time. In one of her letters home, she remarked,

Joe wants to do well. The new girl doesn't; she merely hopes to hold her job. When Joe breaks a dish he is flabbergasted. When the girl does, she tells you about it with a careless laugh, and if you don't show equal lightness, she sulks. We prefer them to be flabbergasted.

That summer Isobel wrote many letters, for she stayed alone at Oak Flat for more than six weeks. Victor and Cath Christianson had to leave, Cath for medical treatment and Victor to hold meetings in Hollow Tree District. And John left for a survey trip made necessary by his new appointment as superintendent of the work in Western Yunnan. To make matters worse—from her point of view—he took along young Lucius, whom she relied on for so many things.

She had other helpers, of course, including the doubtful assistance of Amos (once the Chipmunk). He had improved, but he was still careless when he was supposed to be watching the goats. Just the other night he had come, only slightly shamefaced, to say that panthers had eaten four kids while he was off somewhere else.

When the last of John's carriers had disappeared around a bend in the trail, Isobel felt an unaccustomed weight of loneliness drop around her. Slowly she trudged over to Sunset Ridge and stood looking out across the mountains. It was the time of year when heat mists rose from the canyon, blurring its features with a somber grey film, draining the color from every thing of beauty. No comfort, Isobel thought, not there. Why had God made it such a drab view today? So she would look at Him instead? She turned from the gloomy canyon and asked the Lord to open her eyes to the comfort of His presence.

She decided to occupy herself with preparations for the Rainy Season Bible School coming up in June, and before long she was intent on translating a new hymn. She also started an evening class of basic reading, writing, and hymn singing, "baby lessons," she called them, for a motley group of six young Lisu including the new girl helper, the new cook, Joe, and the goatherd, Amos. She named them the Infant Brigade.

Can you see these six, gathered around our table at evening time, making most awful noises in their effort to learn a new hymn; struggling laboriously with the New Testament letters, and after reading, trying to bend unwieldy minds to the task of getting thought out of those symbols as well as words? Baby lessons, these, but these are foundation days. . . .

In the following weeks, Isobel realized why God had kept her in the canyon. The Lisu Christians were still under a great deal of pressure from the Chinese officials to plant opium, and the heathen took every opportunity to ridicule them for their stand. And the church at Oak Flat needed her now more than ever, for Me-do-me-pa, their "Shepherd," was dying. He had given up his positions as headman and deacon, and he lay in his little shanty, growing weaker every day.

Someone started a rumor that when Me-do-me-pa died, the white missionaries would leave. As soon as Isobel heard it, she assured the Christians that she and John were not leaving, and she took this chance to emphasize that God would never abandon His children, no matter who went away.

Me-do-me-pa himself was troubled about his illness, wondering if he was being punished for some sin he had done. Isobel used the biblical account of Job's experiences to reassure him that suffering is not always caused by sin. During Me-do-me-pa's last weeks, she and Homay took the guitar and climbed the hill every day to visit him and sing his favorite songs.

More than two months had passed since their trip to Luda, and John had returned from his survey when Isobel received a thrilling letter from America. Three frail old ladies, "dear prayer warriors," Isobel called them, had received her letter about the spiritual battle in Three Clans Village. On a certain day they had felt an urgent need to pray about the quarreling clans. Since they were not well enough to travel across town, each lady knelt in her own kitchen and spent the morning in intercession.

"Oh, John," exclaimed Isobel, "I'm going to get my diary. Let's see what the date was." Yes, there it was: March 12; morning in that American town was the same as evening in Lisu country. The ladies had been praying at the very time that God was doing a marvelous thing in the hearts of the clan leaders.

Slowly Isobel closed her diary, thanking the Lord again for His answer to prayer. How the dear prayer warriors would rejoice when they heard what had happened! It was a dramatic illustration of the truth she had seen proven over and over: prayer helpers make a decisive difference in a missionary's fight against the powers of evil.

In that year's Rainy Season Bible School too, Isobel saw the results of friends praying at home. She and John did all the teaching, and they had a good group of students, including representatives from four different tribes. Gad, the converted thief, had returned, bringing a young man from the much-feared Lolo tribe. And with him came the good news of many souls saved in Yongpeh, where he and Daniel had been preaching.

Near the end of RSBS, Me-do-me-pa died. He was buried by the students, and his funeral was a stirring witness for Christ to all the watching heathen.

It seemed to Isobel that the memory of Me-do-me-pa's faithfulness carried over into the consecration service that year. Held at Sunset Ridge around a bonfire of flaming branches, the service was an especially happy time of singing and testimonies. After John's message, the students came one by one to kneel beside him for dedication, bathed in the golden light of the fire. Then the students left, singing as they carried their bright, flickering pine torches into the night. Isobel's heart went after them. How well she knew the trials ahead for those eager volunteers! But they would have plenty of blessings too, and many Lisu souls would be saved because of their ministry.

Homay's husband, Thomas, had been the outstanding student at that school session, and it was decided that he would be the best teacher for Village-of-the-Olives, just across the river. It was a splendid opportunity for Thomas, and of course Homay would go with him, but Isobel and Homay took leave of each other with sadness.

Isobel's regret at parting with Homay was deepened by her concern for the girl's health. Homay still had a strange tiredness that no medicine seemed to help. The Christians at Olives built Homay and Thomas a house and gave them a warm welcome, so Isobel consoled herself with the knowledge that no matter what happened, the young couple would be surrounded by loving hearts.

Gad was another student who had earned the right to take charge of a district all his own, and he was sent to Hollow Tree district, four days' journey to the south, although there was no one to go with him. Hollow Tree was a long distance away, and it was a wide area for a single evangelist to cover, especially one so young. Gad insisted that he didn't mind going alone, but that winter he was much in Isobel's prayers.

Even Amos, the goatherd, seemed to be making progress. He was definitely interested in his books and often studied while he sat with the goats. His voice had developed too: he was one of the finest tenors in the whole church. But he still had not been accepted for baptism because of his careless work. One day after Isobel had paid his wages as usual, she was astounded to hear him mumble that he didn't deserve the money. "Take it back, *Ma-ma,*" he said, obviously embarrassed. She insisted that he keep the money, adding a few remarks about the importance of faithful service; perhaps he would take her words to heart.

For Christmas, Isobel and John decided to make the long trip to Chefoo to visit Kathryn at school. Rynna was nine years old now, and it had been a painfully long time since Isobel had seen her little girl.

On their way south they stopped at Stockade Hill to give a Bible conference that was sorely needed, now that the Lisu New Testament was available. Although the meetings lasted only three days, a hundred students came from all over the district. A young man named Claude dedicated himself to the Lord's work, and Isobel and John happily sent him to help Gad at Hollow Tree. They left Stockade Hill with regret, for the Lisu pleaded for more teaching, but they had to continue their trip east or they would never get to Chefoo in time for Christmas.

The farther they traveled from their mountain stronghold, the more pointedly they were reminded that China was still at war with Japan. At Oak Flat Village they had seen only a few airplanes flying overhead. The heathen Lisu thought they were tiger-demons, and even the Christians stopped work to stare at the strange bird that purred like a hundred tigers and did not flap its wings. Then Thomas had remembered John's description and explained about the Flying House that carried people inside it.

But now Isobel and John saw many airplanes, most of them bombers, and they saw firsthand the roads and bridges that had been destroyed. As they journeyed east, the dangers and uncertainties of wartime so seriously obstructed their attempt to reach the coast that they began to wonder whether they would get there alive. When yet another bridge was bombed before their eyes, they realized that God was closing the door to their plans. They turned back.

Though heart-strings tugged for little girlie, trusting the wisdom of His faithful love who has never failed us in the past, we came back to spend the day with our Lisu children, and their love and welcome certainly comforted us.

By Christmas Eve, 1940, they were back in Oak Flat, caught up in the Lisu's joyous celebration. Isobel searched the faces of those who had come from Hollow Tree. Claude? Yes, he stood with the others next to the welcome arch. But Gad, who had so cheerfully volunteered to work alone at Hollow Tree—where was he?

Claude's face grew solemn as he answered her questions. Early in December he had reached Hollow Tree only to find Gad dying of relapsing fever. Claude told how the heathen Lisu crowded around as Gad calmly declared that he was going home to God. The young evangelist had urged his listeners to obey God, and in spite of all Claude's efforts, had died shortly afterward.

Isobel could hardly believe Claude's report. Not our Gad, she thought. He was so young, so faithful! And he had just begun his ministry. Worse still, Gad's two brothers had come to Oak Flat this Christmas especially to see him. When they heard of his death, one of them became bitterly angry against the Lord.

Since Gad was the first of the RSBS students to die, Isobel and John held a memorial service for him the day after Christmas. Orville Carlson, a missionary who had returned with them, preached at the service that morning. Isobel listened to his words with tear-filled eyes, for Orville's own brother had died while ministering at Luda. Orville had come to take his dead brother's place in the work, and he too had wrestled with questions until the Lord had set his mind at ease. His message was exactly what Gad's grieving brothers needed, and God used it to touch many hearts that day.

Chapter Fifteen

One of the letters Isobel found waiting for her at Oak Flat was a message from Thomas, over at Olives. He wrote that Homay was so sick he hadn't been able to do much traveling away from the village. Immediately Isobel sent a mule to carry Homay back to Oak Flat, hoping that when Leila Cooke returned from furlough she would be able to diagnose Homay's illness.

Homay seemed thinner, but quite at peace, and her face was bright with its usual good humor, so Isobel tried not to worry when Leila couldn't find anything wrong with her. She did suggest that Homay make the trip out to the Chinese hospital, but Homay didn't think she was strong enough to go, even if she rode Isobel's mule.

During the following months and on into the spring of 1941, Isobel thought often of Homay. She might never get well—Isobel shrank from the thought—but please, Lord, she prayed, give her a triumphant heart! Just before RSBS began that year, Isobel went over to Olives to visit Homay for the weekend, and she knew that her prayer was being answered.

Although it was clear that Homay was dying, her thin face shone with love for God. The heathen women marveled at the patient suffering of the young teacher who was not afraid to die, and they often came to talk with her. Everyone knew that Homay's favorite hymn was "Have Thine Own Way, Lord," and she often used its words when she spoke to her visitors.

Because Homay was so ill, Thomas did not come to the beginning of Rainy Season Bible School that year. But one night he arrived just before the evening service, carrying his young son on his back. His eyes were red and swollen, and Isobel knew this could mean only one thing. "When did she die?" she asked through her tears. "How was she?"

Thomas said that Homay's faith was triumphant to the end; her last words were ones of pity for him and their little son. Hardly able to speak for grief, Thomas told Isobel that he just wanted to go away, back to his own village. But he came to class the next day, and before long the little church in Village-of-the-Olives had convinced him to stay and work with them there.

That year more than forty students arrived for RSBS, including two from Goo-moo in Burma; it was the largest school ever. But even while Isobel was busy with services and classes, she pondered the events of the past few months. What a year of dying it had been! First Me-do-me-pa, then Gad, and now Homay. The brightest, the best, the most faithful. Why had God allowed it?

As she worked with the students and watched the heathen who were turning from demon worship, God comforted her heart. A harvest of strong believers had come as a result of that suffering. Multiplied greatly, God would use those believers to reach countless more who had never heard. Whenever Isobel thought about Homay's life—her energy, her skills, her faithful witness—she wondered how many more Lisu girls there might be like her, still waiting to hear the Good News.

Who would go to tell them? Including the Cookes and Orville Carlson, there were now only five missionaries in these mountains. Hundreds of Lisu villages up and down the canyon still had not been reached; hundreds more with believers desperately needed Bible teaching. It would have to be the Lisu Christians who went, and they had many obstacles in their way.

But this was no time to be discouraged, not with the demands of RSBS swirling around her. She sat down and wrote to her prayer partners in America. They already knew and loved Homay; they would want to hear about her triumphant death and how Thomas had courageously preached a resurrection sermon at her memorial service. As a happy footnote, Isobel added the news that Amos, the former Chipmunk, was learning to pray in public and had been accepted for baptism at last. Then she set herself to pray—for both the Lisu young people and those in America—that more young men and women would see the need and offer their lives to God.

Meanwhile, with John away on another trip, what should she do about the opium problem? Even after all this time it had never been properly settled, and during the last week of RSBS, trouble flared up again. The Lisu Christians of the canyon had not sowed opium seed as they had been ordered; they had planted their usual crops of potatoes or wheat. Now the opium commissioner was demanding that the local magistrate collect taxes on all the opium that was supposed to have been grown in the canyon. Even though the Christians had not planted it, they were still required to pay the tax.

Since John wasn't there, the deacons from all over the canyon met at Oak Flat to discuss the problem. First they agreed that they would never plant opium, then they asked Isobel to write on their behalf to Chiang Kai-shek, the president of China, since they had been told that he was a Christian. If he ordered them to pay the opium tax, they would. In the meantime, they set aside June 8 as a day for the whole Lisu church to pray and fast together.

Isobel sent the letter to the president, and she wrote again to prayer partners in America, England, and Australia. The day of fasting came and went, and the summer passed. War news trickled into the canyon: the Japanese had bombed Paoshan, the source of their supplies; 140 Chinese soldiers had arrived at Luchang, where the Chinese magistrate lived. Had they come to fight the Japanese? Or had they come to force the Christians to plant opium?

The heathen Lisu whispered maliciously when the Chinese magistrate arrested Acquila, one of the deacons. They jeered when he was beaten and thrown into prison. Then, infuriated that the lowly Lisu had dared write to the president of China, the Chinese magistrate threatened to use his Chinese soldiers to destroy Plum Tree Village and drive Isobel out of the canyon.

Isobel tried to ignore his threats and prayed all the harder for God to have His way in the situation. It would help so much if John were here to deal with the magistrate, she thought. To the Chinese she was just a worthless woman, and it would only make matters worse if she dared to raise her voice.

At last, on August 26, an answering letter came from the president. Isobel had Lucius translate it and send a copy to each village. The opium order was a mistake, the president said, and he would telegraph the provincial governor right away. Furthermore, he was interested in the tribes of the canyon and was glad to hear that the missionaries were helping them.

Isobel rejoiced with all the church at this good news. Now perhaps the matter would be resolved. By this time John had returned, and he and a group of deacons traveled to the warlord's castle to protest the situation. The warlord was polite but not at all helpful. "I have to collect a certain amount of money from my district," he explained. "And Christians are the only ones with money—the others spend it on opium. But if the magistrate agrees to lessen the tax, then I will too."

At the Chinese magistrate's residence in Luchang, John was received with courtesy and vague promises, then he was dismissed. The deacon, Acquila, remained in prison.

"I knew this wouldn't be a simple matter," John said to Isobel one night, "even with the president's letter in our hands."

Isobel glanced up from the letter she was writing. "There's a lot of money to be made from opium. I've heard that the governor's son is behind those directives. Do you think it's true?"

"I'm afraid so," said John. "It looks like the opium commissioner and the magistrate are all working for him. And our little canyon is so inaccessible that they're pretty sure the central government won't bother them. Besides, the government has its hands full, fighting the Japanese." He bent down to unlace his boots. "We're in for some more trouble."

Two more letters arrived for Isobel and John. One, from a Chinese subofficial, said that John would be held personally responsible for the Christians' refusal to plant opium. The other, from the British consul, rebuked Isobel for getting tangled up in a political affair and warned her that the president's orders would probably never go into effect.

She hadn't made up her mind what to think when she heard that a new manifesto had arrived from the president. She hurried over to read the copy posted in Oak Flat. *ANYONE CAUGHT STEALING WILL BE EXECUTED.* Why didn't it say anything about opium?

She looked at the paper more closely. The original words, *PLANTING OPIUM,* had been pasted over with new words, *CAUGHT STEALING.* Slowly she turned away, automatically following the rocky little path that led to Sunset Ridge. She gazed out over the canyon, and it seemed as drab as the grey-washed sky above. Perhaps the British consul was right: the president had no real power here.

She knew that these anxious days were a time of testing for the Lisu church, and she wished she could give an answer to their anguished questions. Had the day of prayer and fasting accomplished nothing? Why was Acquila still in prison? Some Christians had been forced to give up their cattle because they delayed in paying the tax. Worse still, the governor's son had called for a meeting with all the Chinese magistrates to decide how to punish the rebellious Christians.

But friends around the world were praying, Isobel reminded herself; the church was praying; and each missionary was giving more time than ever to prayer. From Isobel's prayer spot, she could see across the canyon to the ridges and peaks of the other side, and behind one of those ridges lay the town of Luchang, where Acquila was still in prison. "Lord," she prayed, "do Thou Thyself judge these evil men who are inflicting such injustice on Thy children."

God's answer came one evening late in September when the Chinese magistrate and the opium commissioner were eating together. They started to talk about the opium tax, began to trade insults, and suddenly the argument erupted into a fight. The magistrate's father, afraid that his undersized son would be overpowered by the stocky commissioner, snatched up a knife and stabbed the commissioner to death.

Although the magistrate was demoted and made to walk in chains behind the commissioner's coffin, it seemed that the rest of the affair was hushed up. Isobel suspected that the Chinese magistrate had saved his own neck by claiming that he was trying to enforce the president's order.

The church rejoiced on November 11 when Acquila was given his freedom, and again on January 13 when the president's soldiers arrived in the canyon to make sure that all the opium plants were pulled up. The heathen lost their winter crop, but the Christians' crops of wheat and potatoes were safe.

Early in the year of 1942, Isobel decided to try having a Bible school just for girls. Girls had been invited to previous Bible schools, but it seemed that they either dissolved into giggles or concentrated on watching the boys.

Isobel had found the Lisu women especially difficult to reach because they spent all their time working. She also had another obstacle to overcome: even the church deacons expressed their conviction that women just couldn't learn.

In January she made a trip over to Village-of-the-Olives for a short Bible study, and Lucius came along to help with the teaching. The few girls who attended seemed to be brighter and more faithful than any she'd met before, and one in particular was outstanding. The girl didn't have a Bible name yet, so she was just called Third Sister, but Isobel noticed the light on her face as she listened to the Bible messages. Girls like her were exactly the reason for having Girls' Bible School, and Isobel was careful to give her a warm invitation.

Third Sister's heathen father had forbidden her to come, but Isobel tried to encourage her anyway. "Don't give up hope," she said to the girl. "God is able to open your way, and I will join you in prayer about it."

"Thank-you-to-death," Third Sister answered, using the Lisu idiom, and Isobel had to leave it at that.

Although only six girls had signed up so far, Isobel went ahead with her plans. The biggest problem was finding a time when the girls would be free to come. Whenever they weren't farming, Lisu women were spinning, weaving, and sewing for their families. "Perhaps at the Chinese New Year in February," one young evangelist suggested. "If the girls work a little harder before and after, they won't get behind in their sewing."

That settled it for Isobel, and although she hoped for more than six, she arranged to borrow the Chinese school since it would be empty for the holidays. To her delight, twenty-four girls showed up, their faces as bright as the yellow primroses that bloomed among the rocks. And one of those girls was Third Sister from Olives! God had worked a very interesting solution to the problem with her father. That night after the service, Lucius told Isobel what had happened.

Unknown to everyone, he had fallen in love with Third Sister, and just last week he had sent her a like-letter, which to the Lisu is the same as a proposal of marriage. "Don't tell anyone," he cautioned Isobel, then he went on with his tale. Third Sister's father was proud to have such a prosperous, hard-working young man offer to marry his daughter; he would be able to boast of his good fortune to all the village. Naturally, when Lucius asked if Third Sister could come to Girls' Bible School, he agreed.

Isobel was thrilled to hear his secret. Ever since Lucius had started building himself a house over in Olives she had worried about the kind of girl he might choose to marry. But Third Sister would be the perfect bride for him.

"I am giving the girls Bible names," she said to him. "What would you like Third Sister's to be?"

Lucius thought for a minute. "Mary is a nice name," he said finally, and he went off to his work with a beaming face.

For this first school Isobel told the girls stories of Bible women like Leah and Abigail, and they responded with heartfelt interest. Mary always sat right up at the front, a lovely picture of Lisu girlhood, Isobel thought, with her dark hair and rosy cheeks. Along with the regular hymns, Isobel taught them several action songs, thinking that they could have a ministry with the children.

At the closing program, Isobel noticed with amusement that the adults joined heartily in learning the action songs too. To her satisfaction, the church deacons and other men who came were amazed at the messages the girls gave and the verses they had memorized.

When one of the men from last year's Rainy Season Bible School remarked that the program was almost as good as theirs, Isobel had to laugh at him. She thought it was every bit as good. Apparently the deacons did too, for they voted to have a Girls' Bible School every year.

Shortly after the end of Girls' Bible School, Isobel decided that she had to do something about the toothache that had been bothering her for weeks. She had tried treating it with medicine, since the closest reliable dentist lived far away in Kunming, but she couldn't ignore the pain any longer.

Gingerly she rubbed her swollen jaw. Since the Burma Road had been finished, she could get to Kunming in about two weeks, but still, that meant a whole month away. Reluctant as she was to leave Oak Flat, she consoled herself with the thought of seeing John. He was at a conference in Chungking; maybe they could meet at Kunming and return together. That would be wonderful—she hadn't seen him for three months—but meanwhile, she had to do something about this tooth!

Chapter Sixteen

Isobel left early in the morning of March 18 and, already homesick for her Lisu, noticed every detail of the landscape. Although distant peaks were still snowcapped, the mountains through which they traveled had been transformed by spring. Dull brown had turned to tender green, and the rocky slopes were trimmed with pink wild peach blossoms and white rhododendron.

Lucius came along too, since he was still building his house and wanted to buy nails in Paoshan; she was glad for his company. During the long hours in the saddle she enjoyed his chatter about village life, and together they listened for the call of the cuckoo bird, which comes in the spring to tell the Lisu, "Plant corn! Plant corn!"

Isobel was looking forward to staying at the home of Kathryn Harrison, John's sister, while she was in Kunming. But first she had to get from Paoshan to Kunming, and that meant riding in a Chinese merchant truck over the steep and winding Burma Road. The truckers were infamous for their dishonesty, and they were reckless drivers too, a fact Isobel remembered whenever she saw the blackened wreckage of a truck on the cliffs below the road. But this time two American pilots who were driving from Paoshan to Kunming offered to give her a ride, and she accepted happily.

That morning she got up early to have her quiet time, since they were leaving at 5:30 A.M. Sleepily she turned to the story of Jacob's ladder in Genesis 28. The fifteenth verse seemed to come to life as she read it: *And behold I am with thee, and will keep thee in all places whither thou goest, and will bring thee again into this land.*

God's promise for the journey ahead! Now she could face the Burma Road without worrying. She told Lucius about the verse while they packed up her bedding, and as she translated it, his face broke into a grin. "Praise the Lord—He's going to bring you back again!"

Well, of course He will, Isobel thought. Lucius didn't get the same thing out of it that I did, but it's still a precious verse.

For four days she traveled with the airmen, finding them good-natured and courteous companions, and all went well until the car broke down. They waited for hours on a desolate stretch of road, and the Americans made plans to commandeer the next truck at gunpoint, but finally they were picked up by a white man in a jeep. Much of Isobel's luggage had to be left in the car by the side of the road; later, when the Americans returned for the car, her bedroll and clothes had been stolen.

By this time Isobel didn't care about her bedding. Her tooth had stopped aching, but her head hurt and she had dizzy spells; all she could think of was getting to a safe place so she could lie down. To her dismay, the Harrisons' house and garden seemed to be deserted. She was wondering what to do next when a young Chinese girl hurried out to greet her. It was Eva, a Chinese pastor's daughter, who had been left in charge of the house.

"Oh, the Harrison family is away in the country for meetings!" she said in clear English. "But come in; I will take care of you."

Eva turned out to be a capable young woman, and she soon had Isobel settled in bed. During the next week, in spite of Eva's careful nursing, Isobel grew more and more ill. When the Harrisons returned, they didn't know what to do for her and neither did the doctor. Finally he wired John to come at once to Kunming instead of taking the trip to Lashio he had planned.

John arrived on Easter Sunday, April 5, and ten days later, as a last resort he asked the dentist to pull Isobel's bad tooth. It turned out to be the cause of a deadly poison that was spreading through her body, and once it was gone, she began to get well.

Meanwhile, the war news was bad. The Japanese seemed to be making gains all over China. What was happening on the east coast, at Chefoo where Kathryn was in school? Isobel fought down her worry. It had been months since she'd had a letter from Rynna.

Nearby, the British were retreating day by day as the Japanese pushed farther and farther into Burma. The Burmese people were fleeing into Yunnan, the closest Chinese province. Air raid sirens howled over Kunming from time to time, and one day they heard that the Japanese had conquered Lashio, the city John had planned to visit.

Now that Isobel was improving, John left to warn the missionaries who worked in isolated western villages and had no radios. As superintendent, he was responsible for their safety; perhaps he could help them get away before the Japanese arrived.

As soon as Isobel regained her strength, she tried to make plans to get back to her Lisu children, even though the way was blocked by Japanese troops. How frightened they would be, with enemy soldiers coming closer and closer to their canyon! Besides, she'd been gone for almost two months, and it was nearly time for Rainy Season Bible School to begin.

News bulletins and terrifying rumors swirled around the missionaries in Kunming. The Japanese had bombed Paoshan at noon on a market day: 1,500 had been killed. The missionaries in Paoshan had escaped to the mountains, finally arriving at Oak Flat Village. At least someone will be there to teach the RSBS classes, Isobel thought. But oh, how she longed to go back.

Refugees streamed into the city with more bad news: the Japanese were closing in from three directions. Would the whole province of Yunnan fall? John came back to Kunming with missionaries who had narrowly escaped the Japanese. Then he was gone again, to Tali.

NOTHING DAUNTED

Terrible stories circulated about the Japanese treatment of women, and the authorities urged all women and children to evacuate to the north. David Harrison and John were somewhere out in the countryside, so there were only women left in the Harrison household: Kathryn Harrison, a new worker named Evelyn Gibson, Isobel, and Eva. The British and American consuls begged them to take advantage of the truck convoys that were moving north.

On May 16 the news blared a warning: JAPANESE CROSS SALWEEN—ADVANCING ON BURMA ROAD. Surely Yunnan would fall! What should we do? Isobel wondered. Four missionaries who lived in the CIM guest house had already flown out to India. John was still gone, and no matter how much she prayed, the Lord hadn't given her any direction about leaving. Three times in the next day the British consul sent orders: join the Royal Air Force convoy leaving tomorrow morning. How could she refuse to obey? Reluctantly she gave in, still wondering whether she was doing the right thing and worrying about Eva, who would have to stay behind because she was Chinese. At the last minute Eva was allowed to go, and Isobel's spirits rose at this evidence of God's kindness.

For seven long dusty days and six watchful nights, bumping along in the back of the truck, Isobel clung to her verse, *Behold I am with thee. . . .* She talked to the Lord about it, seizing the promise that Lucius had pointed out, *and will bring thee again. . . .*

When the trip finally ended, far to the north in Szechwan Province, she was tired and aching from the jolting ride, and the latest war news sent her into despair. Yunnan had not fallen to the Japanese. Generalissimo Chiang's troops had attacked and had chased them back across the Salween River. But here she was, miles and miles to the north, with no way to get back.

The missionaries in Szechwan received the women kindly and invited Isobel to join in the church work, so she hastily brushed up on her Chinese. But the Szechwan dialect was difficult to adapt to; the heat was over 100 degrees, far hotter than in the mountains; and she had almost no money for her personal needs.

Worst of all was the heart-stopping news from Chefoo: Kathryn's school had been captured by the Japanese. Oh, Lord, spare those innocent children! Isobel cried. She had never felt so desolate. What were the Japanese doing to Rynna? If only she could be there to take care of her, to comfort her, to help her understand what was happening. Lord, You can protect her far better than I ever could, she prayed. Put Your arms around her!

After days of uncertainty, friends sent word that the Japanese were treating the captives kindly. Isobel thanked God for that, but she continued her vigilant prayers.

Her only comfort in the whole situation at Szechwan came from the Lord. He gave verse after verse that strengthened her, assuring her of His love and enabling her to get through one day at a time. *I will bring thee again* echoed through her mind day and night.

When a letter came from John describing his ministry among the refugees in Yunnan, Isobel thought that perhaps now the Lord would fulfill His promise. But the senior missionary in Szechwan was not encouraging. "There is still fighting in Yunnan, isn't there?" he said, looking worried. "Very few trucks are going that way, and the consul would never give permission for you to return."

Isobel wrote to the CIM's general director, but his answer suggested that she wait until John invited her. Another drawback to her hopes was the fact that she would have to pay her own way to Yunnan, and she had no money.

It was all too confusing. Going back without the consul's permission didn't bother her nearly as much as the question of getting clear guidance from the Lord. So she spent the next morning, Sunday, in fasting and prayer, and laid four requests before the Lord: money, a direct invitation from John, trucks going to Yunnan, and maybe even a companion for her trip on the dreaded Burma Road.

The next day, the Lord gave her four specific answers. Two gifts of $50 arrived in the mail, both from the same person but posted six months apart. John sent her a telegram, asking her to join him. A missionary friend located a convoy of three merchant trucks that were headed for Kunming. And Eva begged for the chance to go back with Isobel; she wanted to accompany her to Lisu country and work for her there.

Isobel marveled at the way God had provided the money, but she could hardly believe that He was going to give her Eva too. The girl was such a good helper, such a spiritual companion, so well educated, bright, and cheerful. "Are you sure you want to let me have her?" she asked the Harrisons. Kathryn Harrison explained that she would be working somewhere else and wouldn't need Eva, so Isobel took Eva as an incredible answer to prayer and made plans to pay Eva's fare back too.

By Wednesday they were on their way. Despite the fearsome discomforts of the week-long trip and a truck driver who threatened to abandon them in the mountains, they reached Kunming in safety.

Isobel's only thought was to keep going west to Tali, where John was still working. But David Harrison asked her to teach his Bible class for two weeks so he could make a much-needed visit to his country churches. Isobel clamped down on her impatience and taught the class. Some of the university students asked if she could start morning Bible studies for Christians too. Thank God they were interested! She accepted the challenge and was teaching three classes by the time David Harrison returned to Kunming. Then she hurried on to Tali.

At Tali she found that John had been sent to Paoshan with the Medical Unit, but the day after she arrived, she received letters from both John and Kathryn. John's letter gave her the dismal news that he would not return until August, several weeks away. Kathryn's letter was the first she had received for seven months. It had been written after the Japanese had taken over her school, and its happy chatter did much to quiet Isobel's fears. From Kathryn's comments she could tell that Roxie Fraser, J. O. Fraser's widow, was mothering her little girl during the internment; she would be in good hands.

By this time Isobel was desperately lonely for John, and she tried everything she could think of to get to Paoshan. But Paoshan was now in the military zone, just one day's journey from the front line of battle in the Salween Canyon, and only the Chinese were being given military passes. She even appealed to General Song for a pass, but his soldiers kept her waiting at the outer gate for hours, then sent her home empty-handed.

That evening she received a message from General Song. She could expect her husband back in Tali—soon. God is working, she thought. What is going to happen next?

John did arrive shortly, and the general invited them out to his estate for a lavish banquet. Isobel soon learned the reason for such favor. Although the Chinese had always regarded the Lisu tribes with contempt, the war had suddenly given the "monkey people" strategic importance.

Already the heathen Lisu were helping the Japanese to establish outposts in the canyon, General Song said. He wanted to make sure that the Christian Lisu in the northern part of the Salween Canyon would be friendly to the Chinese cause. He had tried to talk to the Salween warlords but found them interested only in opium. "Opium sots," he called them in disgust. So he had thought of John and Isobel, who spoke both Lisu and Chinese fluently. "Will you help us?" he asked.

Isobel and John assured him that they had already warned the Lisu that the Japanese would destroy their churches, and they agreed to do what they could.

The events that followed amazed Isobel. First they were entertained at a magnificent Chinese feast in General Song's mansion, then John was named adviser to Colonel Hsie, who headed up the Nationalist Guerilla unit in the Oak Flat district. Best of all, General Song gave orders for Colonel Hsie and a military escort to accompany Isobel, John, and Eva to Oak Flat Village.

Despite a truck breakdown on the Burma Road, unrelenting rain, and a long climb through the Salween Canyon, the small group arrived back in Oak Flat Village by the end of August.

Isobel was worn out, but she praised God for what He had accomplished. Six months, she thought, gazing at the dear Lisu faces she had longed for. Six months of being tossed hither and yon, of seeing God strip her of all supports, of seeing Him faithful to His Word, of finding Him *sufficient*. And He had brought her home at last!

She was soon immersed in her work, but she and everyone else were conscious of living in the war's danger zone. The Japanese had set up camp on the west side of the Salween River Canyon, a few days' journey to the south, and Colonel Hsie's guerrillas were busy digging trenches on the east side of the river. Oak Flat Village was also on the east bank, but it was located two thousand feet above the river; perhaps they would not get caught in the crossfire when fighting began.

Chapter Seventeen

In the months that followed, John's duties as adviser to Colonel Hsie and superintendent of the Chinese churches along the Burma Road took him on frequent trips out of the canyon. Conscious of the anxiety felt by the churches, Isobel decided to set an example of the courage and faith that Christians should have. She declared that war or no war, they would carry on their usual program. She even made plans to hold an October Bible School, since the RSBS held while she was away had been cut short by an epidemic of paratyphoid.

School began on schedule one sunny October day, but that Saturday a runner brought frightening news. Soldiers wearing strange uniforms—more than a hundred of them—had arrived at Cow's Hump Village, just north of Oak Flat. Perhaps they were the dreaded Japanese!

The villagers began to pack their meager belongings, and some fled into the ravine. John was away, but four missionaries still remained at the station with Isobel. When they discussed the situation, Isobel was startled to learn that she was the only one not making plans to escape.

Remembering her painful experiences the last time she let someone push her into running away, she said quietly, "I'm not going to go anywhere until the Lord clearly tells me to." And she shared a verse God had given her from Isaiah 26:12, *Lord, thou wilt ordain peace for us.* The married couple decided to get out of the canyon, but the other two missionaries, single men, did not want to leave Isobel alone, so they stayed.

On Sunday, Isobel was glad to see that several hundred Lisu had braved the rumors and gathered for worship; she made sure they knew that Bible school would continue on Monday as usual. Later they found out that the strange soldiers were merely a group of deserters from the Chinese army whose uniforms were different from anything the Lisu had seen.

Rumors! *Wind-words,* the Lisu called them; they could chill a man's courage and shrivel his desire to serve God. Isobel resolved not to let the daunting wind-words hamper their work at Oak Flat. During the Christmas festival that year she talked about Bible school to the girls who had come from all over the canyon. By now Mary and Lucius were married, and two other girls from last year's school were brides as well. "Remember Girls' Bible School last February," she said. "Remember how good it was?" The girls nodded and smiled in agreement; yes, they had enjoyed it, but high taxes had taken all their money—and what about the war? Not one girl signed up to come again.

As the new year of 1943 began and February approached, the missionaries had to decide whether or not to have Girls' Bible School. There was plenty of work that must be done ahead of time: dormitories to repair; new songs to translate; lessons to prepare. After much prayer they agreed that unless the Lord told them otherwise, their motto would be "Business as usual."

John had gone down the canyon to help rescue a missionary couple behind enemy lines, so arrangements were left up to Isobel and Charles Peterson, the young missionary in charge of the station when John was away. Isobel had great plans for the school. She wanted to give the girls some lessons in baby care and general cleanliness since the heathen Lisu thought that sickness was caused by the bite of a demon and had no idea that germs even existed. Eva would help too, and she could teach the girls how to knit.

Saturday, the opening day of Bible school, brought a storm of snow clouds that blew icy rain and dampened Isobel's hopes, but even so, a dozen girls from the east bank of the river straggled in. What about the girls from the west bank, from Olives? They were the best students, both mentally and spiritually, and she had prayed hard for them to come. In this weather? Lucius, who had come early to help set things up, looked worried, for Mary was in that group. Those girls would have to travel more than twenty miles of mountain trails and then try to cross the Salween River in a flimsy raft.

By Monday the rain had let up, although dark, low-hanging clouds still hid the mountain peaks, and at dusk Isobel heard the shout she'd been straining her ears for. "Here come the girls from the west bank!" Mary and ten others—all of them arrived safely. That evening the bad weather closed down again, but the thirty-three students and their two teachers paid no attention to the storm—they were rejoicing together in a service of praise.

Once Girls' Bible School was past, Isobel set her sights on a new project; she wanted to try a Bible school for teen-age boys. These boys were particularly hard to reach since they were the cowherds of the family and often camped out all night with their cattle. But, Isobel thought, if we made it short—only two weeks— and held it in March before the plowing begins, maybe someone else in the family could watch the cattle.

She encouraged herself by thinking about Amos and the progress he had made. He was no longer working as goatherd, for he had saved his wages and bought a farm for himself and his sister and his old blind mother. After all these years, he had become a worthy member of the community and a faithful witness.

More rumors flew back and forth as March 6 approached, the opening day for Boys' Bible School. The Japanese were marching toward the town of Six Treasuries, everyone said—only a day's journey away. The town's postmaster had already fled. Chinese soldiers were stationed at the ferry crossing, ready to destroy the boat at the first sign of the enemy. Then how would the boys get home?

But thirty-six eager cowherds arrived, and the principal of the Chinese school sent his classes too, bringing the total to seventy-six students. Boys' Bible School was a success, in spite of the distractions of wind-words and the war planes that droned back and forth overhead.

The Lisu church deacons had voted to have three one-month sessions of Bible school this year, and Isobel was grateful for the decision, although she had told no one but John that she was expecting a child this summer. She still wanted to help with the Bible teaching. This year they were studying the epistles of Peter, and she pulled out her notes from her Moody days. At the April session, one of the more distinctive faces in her class was Chi-lee, the only student from a remote and difficult area called The Heathen Patch. Isobel was not favorably impressed, but she described the boy for her prayer partners:

A mop of coarse black hair chopped off without regard to order, low brow, small eyes, shapeless wide-spreading nose, dirty white garments like potato sacking, and forever scratching himself . . .

She had learned not to judge her young students too hastily, and, remembering Gad and Amos, she tried to be patient with Chi-lee. She found out that he could read, and he listened attentively to her teaching although he didn't pass the examination. By the end of the month she decided that Chi-lee had done pretty well, considering where he'd begun. He'd had a haircut and a bath, he wore clean clothes, and his face shone with joy. She invited him back to the August Bible School, and he agreed enthusiastically to come.

By August, a baby son, Daniel, had arrived in the Kuhn family. Even though a nurse journeyed in from Tali to help, Isobel had her hands full caring for the new baby. John did most of the teaching that August, but Isobel still tried to keep up with what was happening, and she kept an eye on the students. Where was Chi-lee? she wondered. He had been so eager to come back.

When she asked a Lisu evangelist, he told her sorrowfully that Chi-lee had "gone back to God," the Lisu way of saying that he was dead. She was still trying to find out what had happened when she received a letter that Chi-lee had sent two months before.

Back in his home village, he had started teaching the young people what he had learned and had been persecuted by the enraged heathen. Finally they had burned his house to the ground and driven him out into the wilderness to live. There he had built himself a shelter of branches and had written to Isobel; by the time his letter reached her, he had already caught the dreaded malarial fever and died.

Isobel grieved for Chi-lee and his brave witness. But he was in heaven now, she reminded herself, and the seed he had sown would be blessed, even in The Heathen Patch. Others remained to carry on the work, teachers like Thomas and Luke, and solid, reliable farmers like Amos. But the need was so great!

All during that summer of 1943, the Japanese pushed back the Chinese guerillas who were fighting in Burma, and by the end of October, a Chinese regiment had retreated over the mountains. They camped at Village-of-the-Olives, just across the river and slightly north of Oak Flat Village.

The soldiers occupied the homes of the Christians in Olives, since they were clean and well supplied, and the Lisu had to let them "borrow" whatever might be needed. The colonel decided that Lucius and Mary's house looked like the best in town, so he made his headquarters there.

In spite of the war, November Bible School started on schedule, and it was accompanied by the difficulties that Isobel had learned to expect. Lucius came from Olives to help out, but John was gone again—to a superintendent's conference in Chungking—and Danny had colic. Her problems continued to multiply.

They had left us but one day when Charles came down with what turned out to be rheumatic fever! At the same time our goatherd took sick and also the girl who does the laundry. And the rain came down!

*Then I got word that Colonel Hsie with his
number two wife was coming through, which I
supposed meant that we must entertain them!
What I would do without Eva's help, I didn't know.*

Isobel prayed with Charles about the situation, and the Lord gave them a promise that strengthened her resolve to keep on with the Bible school no matter what: *Thou art my King, O God: command deliverances for Jacob* (Psalm 44:4). The Lord did deliver them: Orville Carlson came down from Luda to do some teaching; Colonel Hsie set his wife up with a house of her own; and Danny's colic improved when Eva helped him get used to drinking goat's milk.

The Christmas festival that year had to be held in two places, one on either side of the river, since Village-of-the-Olives was overrun with Chinese soldiers and the Christians in Oak Flat could not get permission to cross the river. An encouraging number of Lisu came to the celebration, in spite of reports that the Japanese had attacked Luchang, just thirty-three miles away.

*Previously the fighting had been low down, on the
banks of the river probably, so the sound of it had
reached us as muffled and faraway. But Luchang
is on an altitude level with us, only a few miles
away as the crow flies, and the firing sounded very
close. The great rocky crags above us caught up the
cannon roar and grumbled it angrily to one another
until that belch of death seemed a continuous sound
swirling around our heads. It was rather awful.
We wasted a morning packing for flight.
Then, as the next morning greeted us with still
more vivid flames from a third burning village,
we wasted (!) a second hour or so discussing*

*where to flee; then as everything has continued
quiet ever since, and our side say the others have
retreated, we wasted a third hour unpacking to
stay! Such is life in the midst of war.*

A month later, in January 1944, the Japanese had pressed right into the Salween Canyon, and the struggle for Luchang began the Year of Impossibles for Isobel and John. With the enemy at their doorstep, with gunfire rumbling in the distance, it would be impossible to have Girls' Bible School this February, wouldn't it? John was sick with influenza; Charles Peterson had been sent out on sick leave; Danny still needed his mother's care. And everyone thought the girls would never dare to come.

But John's health improved, and he managed to get a military permit for the girls, so they came despite Isobel's fears. Including faithful Mary, there were twenty-five of them, bright eyed and eager to see *Ma-ma*'s amazing baby with its white skin and downy red hair. Isobel took advantage of their curiosity to provide lessons in what she called "mothercraft."

She invited three or four girls to visit her each morning during Danny's bath time. While they watched him kick and splash in the water, she pointed out that good food, cleanliness, and fresh air were important for all babies. The girls giggled and squealed at the sight of a white baby enjoying himself in a tub of water, but Isobel didn't mind. Perhaps the memory would help them to give their own babies a healthier start in life. Mary seemed especially interested in the lessons, and Isobel knew why: Lucius and Mary were expecting a baby this fall.

Isobel's next Impossible was Boys' Bible School in March. Charles Peterson was still not back; John had gone again; and she was the only white missionary left to do the teaching. Furthermore, she had no pencils or paper left. When she explained the difficulties to the Lisu deacons, she was encouraged by their determination to keep on with the school. They would send her two native evangelists, Luke and Thomas, for the whole month of March, they promised. "All right," said Isobel, "and we will trust God for the writing supplies."

But the opening day of school came and Thomas did not arrive; neither did the boys from the west bank of the river. There still were no pencils or paper.

When she found out that Thomas and the boys had been refused a military pass for crossing the river, she and Luke decided to make a point of praying that God would deal in a special way with this particular discouragement from Satan.

As we prayed for Thomas' release, the Lord worked! Prepare for a surprise . . . into our home here drop some American soldiers. (Whether they dropped from the sky or came in by the road, the censor would not let me tell you.) But after a good square American meal (the poor fellows had not seen such food, simple as it is, for a long time, and wasn't it fun "stuffing" them!) they asked if they could do anything for us, and as they have influence, we got them to pull the proper wire and the evening of the fifth day of school, Thomas arrived. Then blessings avalanched.

The next morning paper and pencils arrived, and so did Charles Peterson, healthy once more. Isobel hadn't had time to compose a new chorus, but she suggested a tune to Luke and he thought up some words with a military theme and everyone enjoyed it. So Boys' Bible School, once thought impossible, turned into a triumphant experience for more than thirty boys—and their teachers.

Fighting between the Japanese and the Chinese guerillas in the Pien Ma Pass continued all summer, but John was able to make it back into the canyon. Wonderful news came from the outside world: Kathryn had been repatriated—set free from the Japanese internment camp—and sent back to America with the other CIM children. The Sutherlands, old friends of the Kuhns, would care for her until they could get back to America.

Isobel tried to curb her longing to drop everything and start for the United States that very minute. RSBS was coming up; they would stay and help Charlie Peterson, then take their furlough after RSBS ended. She'd see Kathryn in just a few more weeks.

The regular Rainy Season Bible School proceeded as planned. Lucius was a good helper and teacher, and Eva began a new ministry with the children, teaching them songs and stories as she gathered them together each day for their own special Bible club.

One memorable day Lucius heard good news from Olives: he now had a baby son. He tossed his black curls with joy, and after consulting with John, named the baby Paul. When little Paul fell suddenly sick, John was able to get Lucius a military pass, and he hurried across the river with medicine from Isobel's supply. Soon he sent back a happy report: baby Paul was doing fine.

So the misty, rainy days of summer blew past, some more difficult than others. The missionaries learned to press on with their work in spite of wind-words that whispered, "It's impossible."

Finally autumn came, and it was time for Isobel and John to leave on their furlough. While she packed, Isobel asked herself, Have we really been gone for seven years? And how can I bear to leave my Lisu children? But she had to admit that she was exhausted; if she wanted to keep on with the work, she would have to get some rest. Besides, she couldn't wait to see Kathryn.

With both regret and anticipation Isobel and John began their long trip out to the coast. First came the steep, roller-coaster trails, now so familiar. On the way they passed the lonely mountain grave of La-ma-wu, the first Lisu evangelist, and Isobel stopped on that high ridge to look back.

Behind her lay the cloud-wreathed mountains, their bumps and knobs and rocky outcroppings dotted with frail Lisu huts. Many who lived in those huts—twelve hundred of them now—belonged to Christ. How glad La-ma-wu would have been, she thought. God had blessed, not a hundredfold, but a thousandfold already.

Chapter Eighteen

Isobel soon realized that traveling with a young child to America during wartime was not the best way for tired missionaries to recuperate. After riding for several days in a crowded, dirty train, they caught a flight to India, waited there for three weeks, then finally obtained cramped quarters in a troop ship that took thirty-six days to sail across the Pacific Ocean.

They docked in California, telephoned to Kathryn in Pennsylvania, and hurried cross-country by train to see her. Danny finally met his big sister, and at last Isobel could throw her arms around her little girl and hold her tightly. Kathryn was thirteen now, almost grown up, but to Isobel's relief, they didn't feel strange with each other. They were a complete family again.

Six months of travel and deputation meetings left Isobel exhausted, but just when she was beginning to wonder whether she'd ever feel well again, the Lord provided them with a house of their own in Dallas, Texas. It was close enough to a school so Kathryn could walk, and it even had a fenced-in back yard for Danny. While John took some seminary refresher courses, Isobel caught up on the rest she needed, and they both enjoyed having students in their home for Bible study and prayer.

When World War II ended and passports to China were once again available from the State Department, John and Isobel received a letter from CIM Headquarters. China was still too dangerous for women and children to return, but the Mission was requesting that superintendents go back early—a year ahead of their families.

Isobel looked at John, remembering the motto that had challenged them all of their married life—GOD FIRST. Even though their happy family circle in Dallas would be broken up, she agreed that he should go. The Lisu must have suffered terribly during the war, and some of them might be more open now to the gospel. It would be an excellent opportunity for John.

The Lord would continue to take care of her and Danny and Kathryn. And it would mean a whole extra year with Kathryn. Her heart leaped at the thought.

The book that Isobel had written on her last furlough, *Precious Things of the Lasting Hills,* had been well received, and it seemed that this quiet year might be a good time to begin another. She would write about Lisu Christians who had been freed from their slavery to demons and still suffered fierce opposition from Satan because of their faith. She titled her new book *Nests Above the Abyss.*

The months passed quickly, and soon it was fall in 1946, time to go back to China. The hardest part was leaving Kathryn behind, another knife thrust to the heart. But Isobel committed her pain to God, and she made arrangements for Kathryn to stay once more with the Sutherlands in Philadelphia. Then, with the sight of her daughter's tear-stained face etched in her memory, she took three-year-old Danny and boarded an ancient freighter bound for China.

They met John in Shanghai, and after a happy reunion, Isobel and Danny flew inland to Kunming, where Lucius waited to join them. Meanwhile, John drove to Kunming with their baggage, a long, dangerous trip across China's bombed-out bridges and roads. After John arrived, they traveled on to Tali, stopping there to encourage Eva, who was taking nurses' training. Then they hurried to Paoshan for supplies. Since John would be detained in Paoshan,

Isobel persuaded him to let her and Danny go on ahead to Lisu country; Lucius would escort them, and they would be fine.

The mountain trail wasn't any easier than Isobel remembered. Their sleeping places were as primitive as ever—one night it was a hayloft, another a deserted corn bin—but the mountainside was washed in golden sunlight, and she could fill her lungs with the crisp, pine-scented air that blew down from snowy peaks. Soon she would see the dear ones she had prayed for during the past two years, and her anticipation shortened the long days of climbing.

The trail seemed oddly deserted; many of the small villages looked abandoned. She asked Lucius for a reason. "People have moved away from the main road because of bandits," he explained. "Many men who used to be soldiers have turned to robbing instead."

The Chinese coolies agreed, noisily. "Yes, this is a dangerous road to travel," they complained. "And the loads are much too heavy."

Although the grumbling continued, Isobel tried to rally them by promising that when they reached the canyon, Lisu helpers would help carry the loads and give them a good meal. Sure enough, they met Lisu Christians at the foot of the last steep ridge. And they'd brought horses! Even Danny rode a horse with two Lisu walking beside him, and he called happily to Isobel about the bumpy ride and the bells on his horse.

At Oak Flat they received a loving welcome, complete with plenty of cold water for drinking and hot water for baths. What a luxury, after five long days on the trail! Among those happy faces were several of the girls from Girls' Bible School, and Mary had sent a loving note from Olives.

But discouragement awaited Isobel too. Their house, for one thing.

The poor old shanty (now twelve years old) was a dilapidated sight—it leaned toward the precipice very distinctly and its thatched roof had been blown off in great patches. Inside, the furniture looked rougher than even memory could recall, and everything was covered with dust and debris. . . .

Isobel didn't mind the rough living; she was used to that. It was the signs of spiritual decay in the church that hurt. While she was writing her book and remembering Satan's attacks on the Lisu believers, she had warned herself that he would lay seige to the young church while the missionaries were away. Even so, it grieved her to see that some Lisu Christians had turned back to the heathen ways of immorality. And two former church leaders had actually broken into the House of Grace to steal what they could.

There were others, true Christians, who had stood firm during the war and the suffering of a six-month drought. To these faithful ones, Isobel turned her attention.

As they crowded in to see me day by day, many a little tale of poverty and suffering, and a warm hand-squeeze of gratitude that once more we have come to help them, made me praise God for the privilege of being here again.

They have indeed suffered. Their clothing is ragged and the dearth of rain killed vegetables and such. They brought love-offerings as Lisu have always done, but they were almost all eggs, as there was nothing else to bring. Corn from last year's harvest fed the chickens. Over a hundred eggs were given us in just a few days.

On Sunday more than 300 Lisu from the surrounding mountains came to worship at the church service. Isobel had carried in a record player, and they especially enjoyed listening to records of vocal quartets and the "Hallelujah Chorus." They were fascinated by Kathryn's old baby doll, which could open and shut its eyes, and by Danny's toy train, complete with fire-spouting chimney and a ringing bell.

Isobel closed her first letter home with a sober request for help:

Pray for us that we may fulfill His purposes in this place. Thieves are plentiful over the whole district— they say the new laird [warlord] nourished them. Pray that we may be enabled to work in peace.

There was good reason for Isobel to be concerned about bandits; reports said that sixty of them were working in the district where she lived. At first she and Danny slept alone, but one night she heard a birdcall right under her window, then an answering whistle from behind the house. Bandits! She lay frozen, praying, for a long time. The next day she learned that three men of the church had trailed the attackers and frightened them off.

After that, a Christian man with his gun slept in the Kuhn's house every night until John arrived. For safety's sake, Lucius invited her to move across the river to Olives, but water and fuel were difficult to get there, so she didn't want to consider it.

Finally, after a three-month delay, John arrived—just in time for the summer's Rainy Season Bible School. The students came hiking up the trail, one by one, or in happy, chattering pairs, until the group was so large that they had to use the Chinese schoolhouse.

Since children's work was virtually unknown in the area, Isobel taught the student-evangelists about the importance of Sunday schools and Bible clubs for young Lisu boys and girls. By the end of the summer, the students were fired up with enthusiasm and scattered to their home villages to pass on the teaching they had received.

Isobel and John had returned from furlough with renewed determination that the Lisu church be well equipped to teach its own people. Although World War II was over, the Communists were already fighting with China's Nationalist government for control of the country. What would happen to the Lisu church if the Communists took over? All missionaries would be forced to leave, since the Communists considered it a weakness to believe in any kind of God. And certainly the Lisu Christians would be persecuted. Now was the time to ground them well in God's Word so they would be strong enough to stand alone.

During the next year, however, the church at Oak Flat Village seemed to be sliding further and further away from spiritual strength. Keh-deh-seh-pa had replaced the beloved Me-do-me-pa as headman, and he cared only for wealth and political power. Worse still, the church deacons did not dare to oppose him.

From time to time, Keh-deh-seh-pa's followers tried to gain more power by placing a certain man as schoolmaster or as pastor for this village or that. They wanted the missionaries to support their choice, and they often threatened Isobel when John was away. Twice, when their candidate was an unprincipled, immoral man, she refused to give her approval. The few loyal Christian men in the village tried to protect her, but small, unexplained misfortunes kept happening to her flock of goats and her water supply.

These are not just accidents, Isobel thought. And if I don't cooperate, it's going to get worse, especially with John gone so much of the time. When Charles Peterson returned from furlough to head up the work, matters improved, but Isobel could see that Oak Flat Village was becoming a dangerous place for her and Danny to live.

The next RSBS, during the summer of 1948, was as well attended as ever, and included one group of students that traveled all the way from Burma. A guest speaker continued Isobel's emphasis on reaching the Lisu children, and God worked in many hearts. As the students made their plans for the future, Isobel had great hopes for a far-reaching ministry that would spread up and down the canyon.

But the jubilation of Closing Day was spoiled by fighting. A crowd of Keh-deh-seh-pa's followers who wanted a certain ungodly man named as a pastor started a quarrel with Christians who did not. Although John intervened and no blood was shed, he and Isobel were heartbroken that the church in Oak Flat had become so weak. How could the heathen ever be won if they saw the Christians feuding with each other?

I may never know why God allowed this, Isobel thought, but I'm going to claim Philippians 4:6—*Be careful (anxious, fretting) for nothing.* She resolved to commit the whole incident to God and to seek His guidance for what to do next. For one thing, He had made it clear that they should move to Olives.

Lucius was delighted. "I'm going to build you a house right next to mine," he exclaimed. "Mary will be so glad! We can haul in firewood for you and later we'll make charcoal. And I've been thinking about the water. We could fix up a bamboo pipe to bring water in from the water hole during the night."

By December, Lucius had finished the Kuhns' new home at Olives. It was well thatched and had three rooms with braided bamboo mats for walls. There was a kitchen, a storeroom, and a central room that they could use as a dining room, study, medical dispensary, and guest room. Isobel, John, and Danny would sleep in a loft up over the storeroom.

The house was smaller than House of Grace and it was right in the noisy center of Olives, but it was safe and God had led them there, so Isobel was content. She found that living in Olives gave them a chance to reach out to certain heathen families that they'd had no contact with before.

Because of the problems at Oak Flat, they decided to hold the next year's RSBS at Olives, and Lucius spent the first two months of 1949 building a five-room adobe house that would be large enough to use as schoolhouse and dormitory for a hundred Lisu students. John had to make a trip to Paoshan for supplies, but he planned to be back in time for the school.

The sunny days of February drifted into the peach blossom days of March, and still John had not returned from Paoshan. RSBS was to be early this year, from March to May, and he had wanted to help with the teaching, but now it didn't look likely. What has happened to him, wondered Isobel. She'd heard rumors that the Communists were causing problems near Paoshan. Had they arrested John?

RSBS began, and still he had not returned. Finally a smuggled letter reached her, brought by a villager who had gone to the market at Luchang. The man must have seen the relief on Isobel's face as she read it, for he said, "*Ma-pa* is safe, then?"

"Yes," Isobel said. "The Communists are attacking Paoshan, so he can't get out. But he says the people are so frightened that they are willing to listen to him talk about God."

The man's eyes widened. "Communists! I have heard that there are outlaw bands all through these mountains working for them."

Isobel nodded. "It seems to be their plan. They send in bandits to terrorize a place; then the army comes to liberate the people and they take over."

She and Charles Peterson kept on with the school and tried not to think about the Communists. One weekend when the students had gone out to preach in the villages, a man from Olives made the half-day trip to Luchang to sell his corn, and he rushed back with frightening news.

"Communist bandits," he gasped. "Thirty of them at Luchang! The Chinese magistrate has already run off to Burma."

Lucius looked up from his typing and frowned. "I have heard that they are part of a larger group that attacked Six Treasuries," he said. "They surprised the warlords and made off with thousands of dollars."

"Yes," said the villager, "and now this band in Luchang says they are coming down to Olives." He shot a glance at Isobel. "I don't know what for, unless they're after the missionaries. Or maybe the headman; he has some guns."

"What?" Lucius jumped to his feet. "Their leader is Dai Yi-gwan. He is a fiend, a mad dog! I'm going to get Mary and Paul and the others to hide up in the cave. You and Danny should go too, *Ma-ma;* you know how he hates you."

Both men hurried off, but Isobel sat still for another minute. Dai Yi-gwan? Years ago, when she had caught him trying to cheat the Lisu, she had embarrassed him in front of the whole village. He had hated her ever since, and he would take his revenge.

Chapter Nineteen

Isobel decided not to go into hiding, but she tucked away some medicines and kerosene where they couldn't be stolen, and she prayed. Rain began to fall that night, and it soon became a deluge. Day after day for two weeks the rain kept up, although it was much too early for the rainy season to begin.

The tributaries of the Salween River swelled into roaring cataracts of water, and everyone knew that the bandits in Luchang would not dare to cross the stream between them and Olives. But the rain didn't stop RSBS. Isobel, Charles Peterson, and their students listened to the steady downpour on the roof and thanked God for His protection.

As the school sessions continued, rumors and news flew up and down the canyon. Isobel learned that Dai Yi-gwan was leading the bandits that had stayed on the east bank of the Salween. They had invaded Oak Flat Village and had made a point of asking where she was. The headman, Keh-deh-seh-pa, had joined the band, and they had gone off to rob Dwan, the young warlord. Dwan had outwitted them, however, and had killed more than twenty outlaws with hand grenades from his secret arsenal.

Dai Yi-gwan had escaped with his life, only because he was *gwa-cho,* a covenant friend of Dwan's. Keh-deh-seh-pa had fled to the mountain caves, but reports said that Dwan had sent spies to find him, planning to skin him alive. Isobel shuddered to think about this brutal heathen punishment for Keh-deh-seh-pa. If only he would turn back to God before it was too late! That would take a miracle, she thought doubtfully, but I will pray for him anyway.

Although Chinese soldiers forced the bandits to retreat, Communists still controlled the canyon just north of Olives. The warlord Dwan moved into Olives, considering it the best place to take a stand against the Communists, and his presence caused a great deal of hardship for the Lisu. The warlord and his retinue—seventy of them—demanded food to eat, tables, and other supplies.

Isobel listened sympathetically to the complaints of the Christian Lisu. They were especially hard-pressed since they were not as poor as the heathen and were more reliable. They must run messages, their master ordered; they must carry baggage; they must guard the rope bridge; they must dig trenches—right through the cotton field that belongs to Lucius's mother! All this was to be done without pay, since they were only serfs. Now who was left to hoe the corn and watch the cattle?

The demands made on those who lived with Lucius were all the heavier since Mary was sick now and could not carry loads for Dwan like the other women did. Timothy, her young nephew, was sent in her place, leaving only the old mother at home with Mary, and Lucius had to care for the farm as best he could between his other duties.

Meanwhile, the warlord cut all rope bridges across the Salween except the one at Olives, then he moved two machine guns into the village to await an attack from the Communists. One day a runner brought news that Isobel's old enemy, Dai Yi-gwan, had escaped from Dwan's *yamen* (castle) and had been shot to death on his way to join some other outlaws. Isobel thanked God for delivering her and continued to pray that somehow Keh-deh-seh-pa would turn back.

RSBS ended, summer slipped away, the work of the church went on, and John finally returned from the Communist siege of Paoshan. He did not stay long. Supplies of their Lisu books were beginning to run out, and he couldn't put off a trip to Kunming for reprints, since books like *First Steps in Reading* were essential to the ministry. Besides, the Christmas festival was coming up, and many who came in from distant villages would be counting on finding the books there.

As Christmas approached and John had still not returned, Isobel could only assume that he had been caught in another uprising. Before long the Communists will control this whole area, she thought. And then I'll wish I had taken Danny out of the country. But how can we get away? The usual route through China was already closed. The only other way was through the mountains of Burma, over the Pien Ma Pass, then down through the Burmese jungles to the seacoast.

Besides the threat of communism, Isobel had another reason for wanting to take six-year-old Danny to America. She could not insist that he play only with Christian children, and he was old enough now to pick up heathen words and ideas from his friends. She had tried to get him into the mission school at Kunming, but fighting between Nationalist and Communist armies blocked the way.

So—sometime soon—they must go, she decided, and it would have to be through Burma. She wrote to Mission headquarters about her predicament, asking them to contact the American Baptist Mission at Myitkyina in Burma, in case she needed money when she got there, and she began saving the silver coins she would have to use for paying carriers on the way.

Meanwhile, she and Charles Peterson went on with preparations for the three-day Christmas festival, set to begin on Friday, December 23. That Monday, December 19, Isobel was handed a warning note from a Christian Lisu who was working with the Communists.

> *Dear Ma-ma—We are coming down to 'liberate' Olives this week. Do not be afraid. I will be there in person and I have my men under control. Do not try to run and do not hide your things. You will not be harmed at all, I promise you. I hope to pass Christmas with you all. The writer is—*
>
> *"Red Thomas"*

Isobel read the note again and shook her head sadly. Red Thomas actually thought the Communists would cure China's troubles. He knew nothing of politics—if only she could help him see the truth! But it was kind of him to warn her. Or was this a ruse to keep her from getting away?

Soon after, a church deacon slipped into her house and whispered that he had seen Communist troops close by, at Lameh. "Red Thomas is with them," he added, "and they are bringing the *Lo-zi-lo-pa* also, to help fight Dwan."

The *Lo-zi-lo-pa!* Isobel had heard terrible stories about the cruelty of those heathen Lisu bandits. Once she had met an old woman whose goats they had stolen. Before they left her, the *Lo-zi-lo-pa* pounded the woman's hand to a pulp against a rock, then tied her up in the river. And now those same outlaws were on their way to Olives.

"No one controls the *Lo-zi-lo-pa,*" Lucius said, gazing at her anxiously. "Do you think you should try to get away from Olives?"

Isobel didn't know what to say. She was more worried about the Christians in Olives—how they would suffer! Shouldn't she stay with them? If only John were here! What did the Lord want her to do? "I will ask the Lord," she said simply.

She went upstairs to their little loft and sat down with her Bible. After a while God gave her a promise from Malachi 3:17— *my jewels . . . I will spare them, as a man spareth his own son that serveth him.*

"I think we will be kept," she told Lucius.

His face was troubled. "But *Ma-ma,* how can you be sure of these things? Many times I have seen you pray, and then you find a good verse, but how—" He hesitated.

"How do I know it's really from God and not just my imagination?" Isobel smiled at his embarrassment. "I guess I've learned to wait for Him to speak to me. But He guides in different ways. Sometimes a verse will spring to life as I read it. Sometimes when I'm praying, I will have the sense that I should do one thing or another. And when I do what He wants me to, He gives peace of heart, no matter what else is going on."

Lucius nodded. "I have seen you with that peace." Then he looked wistful. "Sometimes God gives me a verse too, but I wish He would speak to me like He does to you."

"He will, as you keep on listening and wanting to obey," Isobel said. "Learn to hear Him in the small things first and His voice will be clear when you have a big decision to make."

"Like now—with the *Lo-zi-lo-pa* coming?" But Lucius no longer looked worried.

"Yes," Isobel said. "I don't have any peace about leaving, and the Lord gave me that verse. I'm going to hide the medicines, but otherwise I will make no preparation. Let's keep on praying."

Wednesday afternoon, Lucius stopped in to give Isobel the latest news. "Five Communists here!" he said angrily. "They say we must prepare food for 180 men—coming tonight. The headman has already hidden his guns." He thrust a folded paper at her. "Here's something from Red Thomas."

He was gone again, but he returned at dusk and convinced Isobel to move into his big two-story mud house, since its thick walls were bulletproof. She gathered up Danny and went, even though Red's note was just as reassuring as the first.

"There's going to be a battle here tonight," Lucius said. His voice dropped to a whisper. "Dwan is setting up an ambush."

That night they heard only three gunshots and Thursday passed quietly. When they woke up on Friday morning, Christmas Eve, the Communists had moved into the village, and Red Thomas had taken over the house belonging to Lucius's father. Lucius tried to warn him about Dwan, but Red had his scouts on the hilltops and did not seem worried.

That afternoon, the headman's voice rang through Olives. "Every man to your house! Stay off the road."

He must have gone to get Dwan, thought Isobel as machine-gun fire rattled through the trees. She and Danny crouched in Lucius's house with Mary and the rest of the family. Shots echoed from the rocky cliffs, and the fighting went on for four hours. When it was over, Dwan had won back the village and Red Thomas had escaped, disguised by a Lisu turban. Several Communists were dead, and the rest of them had disappeared into the hills.

That evening a runner from the south brought a government document for all the warlords. The governor of Yunnan had yielded the whole province to the Communists; everyone must submit to the new regime.

Overnight Dwan decided to become a Communist, and he withdrew his soldiers from the village. But now the Communists were furious at the resistance they had met in Olives, and they sent word that they were going to allow the *Lo-zi-lo-pa* to plunder and kill as they chose.

Hurriedly Dwan drafted letters proposing a peace conference, and once again Isobel's friends urged her to escape into Burma while she could. But John still hadn't returned, and she had no peace about leaving. That very morning the Lord had given her a verse from Ecclesiastes 10:4—*Leave not thy place.*

So the Christians of Olives prayed, and they posted scouts to warn of the *Lo-zi-lo-pa* attack. Day after day passed with no news. Then they learned that the warlord's messengers had arrived just in time to keep the *Lo-zi-lo-pa* from starting out. There would be a peace conference, and no revenge would be taken upon the village.

Now that the whole province had fallen to the Communists, Isobel knew she had to get Danny to a place of safety. If she was going to try to get out through Burma, her Lisu friends warned, she would have to go soon, before the February snows closed the high passes.

Still, the Lord had given her no direction about leaving. And she couldn't forget what had happened in 1942 when she ran away to Szechwan. Besides, where was John? How could she leave the country without seeing him again?

December faded into the new year of 1950, and still she waited.

One day early in January, a signal flashed up the mountain from the Lisu outpost. *Someone coming!* Isobel hurried outside and scrambled up onto the high rock that they used for a lookout. Two climbing figures came into sight, with a line of carriers winding back behind them. Could it be—? She shaded her eyes to see better. Yes! It was John—and Eva too. She slid off the rock with a glad cry and ran down the trail to meet them.

There was so much news to catch up on! John had been cut off by fighting on the Burma Road, but he brought hundreds of books with him—books so badly needed, so eagerly awaited. Eva had graduated from nurses' training and had come to give the Lisu all the medical help she could.

When Isobel mentioned her concern about Danny, John frowned. "Yes, I've been thinking about Danny too. I guess you should try to get him out to America as soon as possible." Then he brightened. "But maybe if we hurry, you can get back into China before the Communists are organized enough to clamp down on this area."

Isobel nodded. Oh, how she hoped she could!

Shortly after that, she heard a surprising report about Keh-deh-seh-pa. He had sent a large gift to Dwan, along with apologies and protestations of innocence, and had been granted a pardon. While she and John were still discussing this news, Keh-deh-seh-pa himself arrived at Olives.

On Sunday he appeared before the church, confessed his sins in public, and made an apology to the church and to John. The deacons met with him in the Kuhns' house, and after he had made his confession, they asked Isobel if she would like to question him too.

The man apologized to her, but she was still worried about him, so she challenged him to make sure he was really saved. For the first time, he looked truly ashamed and stopped making excuses for his actions. "I believe that Jesus died for my sins and He has forgiven me," he said. "I believe I am born again, *Ma-ma*."

When Keh-deh-seh-pa was finally restored to fellowship, all the church rejoiced. "Just a year ago he seemed like a hopeless case!" Isobel exclaimed to John. "God has truly done a miracle in that man's heart." She smiled, remembering how she had prayed for him without much hope that he'd ever change. I'm glad I was here to see this happen, she thought. If I'd hurried to escape to Burma, I would have missed it.

As February approached, there was no doubt in anyone's mind that Isobel and Danny should leave soon, but John suggested holding one last Bible school and Isobel agreed with enthusiasm. Quickly they made preparations, and to their joy, a hundred Lisu came. On weekends when the students traveled out to work in the northern villages, many more Lisu turned to the Lord. Eva ministered to countless sick men and women, and she became known far and wide for her medical skills. Isobel and John agreed that it was the most heartening, most blessed Bible school they had ever held.

When the school ended, it was already late in February, and Isobel couldn't put off leaving any longer. John wanted to accompany her on the two-week trip through Burma, but she convinced him to stay and teach the hundreds of new Christians who needed him. Lucius offered to go with her, and John arranged for dependable Lisu carriers so she would be well cared for.

Nothing much had happened in the Salween Canyon since the Communists had taken over, but everyone knew it was only a matter of time. Already, missionaries in central China were forced to escape for their lives, and mission stations were being closed by Communist persecution.

Early one morning, Isobel stood at the door of her house and gazed out across the dear, familiar scene. Peace lay across the village, tangible as the wood smoke that curled above each shanty. If only it could stay like this always, she thought. If only I could stay forever.

She pondered the latest news. John had hoped she could return to the Salween Canyon, but she was sure now that the Communists would not let her back in. I will never see this place again, she thought. She stepped back into her house and tried to concentrate on packing. "Remember that this is the Lord's work," she told herself. "He will care for it."

The last few days went too quickly, and soon it was time to say good-bye to Eva and her Lisu family. And to John. This time he could not smile, but when she turned for one last glimpse up the trail, he stood high on the lookout rock, and he was waving.

Chapter Twenty

Pitter-patter. Pitter-patter. Pitter-pat. Isobel sat up and stared into the predawn darkness. Rain on the roof here meant snow on the mountaintop. After three days of climbing the rocky slopes of Pien Ma Mountain, she had hoped that today they would cross the great Pass itself.

She glanced at Danny, sleeping beside her, then across the ashes of last night's fire to the plank bed where Lucius and Caleb were already stirring. She sighed. The route over the Pass was nothing more than a narrow cow path; snow would make it impossible to find, and if the snow didn't stop soon, the Pass would be closed. She curled back into her sleeping quilts and began to pray.

It rained all that day and all night and all the next day. Isobel and her Lisu carriers, eleven of them, took turns amusing Danny in the small cabin that was already crowded with sooty cupboards and oddments of junk. They listened to the endless dripping of the rain and they talked. Isobel thought about the time God had used rain to keep the bandits away and tried to control her impatience.

"Looks like a ten-day rain," one man finally said. "The Pass will be closed by now. Should we go back?"

Isobel eyed him, wondering how to answer. Go back? But when the Communists took over, that would mean imprisonment or worse—and the Communist official was due to arrive in Luchang next week.

"Not yet," she said. "Let's keep praying." She remembered the prayer for guidance she had used so often in the face of trouble: Lord, she prayed silently, if this obstacle is from Thee, I accept it; if it is from Satan, I refuse it. Please show us what to do.

As she waited, an idea came to her. She gave the carriers an encouraging smile. "If it's not raining when we wake up tomorrow, let's take it as a sign that we should start up to the Pass. Then we'll go as far as we can and ask God to show us what to do next."

The next morning Isobel was awake and listening at dawn. There was no pattering on the roof. Could it be? She jumped up to look out the door. Dark clouds hung low on the mountain peaks around them, but for the moment, it was not raining.

Lucius was up too, making a fire for breakfast. "We'll never be able to find the trail—not after two days and nights of snow," he said quietly. "Many people have died trying to cross Pien Ma in snowtime."

Isobel nodded. "I know. If we have any trouble, we'll turn back. But let's go see." She had to make him understand. "It's not raining—not right now—and that's what I asked God for."

Lucius prodded the doubtful carriers into action, and the man who owned the cabin kept warning them about the dangers ahead, but finally they set out toward the top of Pien Ma. Isobel rode Jasper, and two Lisu men carried Danny on a canvas mountain chair.

It took the whole morning to climb through a dark and lonely forest of overhanging trees. Isobel remembered coming this way on their trip to visit Goo-moo, but then she'd had John beside her and sunny skies overhead. Now the clouds seemed to press closer than ever and a cold, drizzling rain began to fall.

After a while the rain stopped, but by then they were climbing through thick clouds that enveloped the mountaintop. It was hard to see ahead, and moisture clung to everything; water even beaded up on Jasper's mane and dripped off the packs carried by the plodding, grim-faced Lisu. Isobel began to wonder whether she was endangering all their lives. Should we turn back, Lord? she prayed as Jasper struggled up the rocky slope. What should I do?

A shout pierced the fog, up ahead. Two dark figures hurried toward them through the gloom. Traders! They must have just climbed over the mountain. Isobel's carriers called to them: "How's the snow on the Pass?"

"It's deep, but our footprints are deep too; they will show you the path," a man called back. "If you hurry."

Everyone walked faster now, anxious to get to the top. Soon they met two more men from the same group. "It's beginning to snow again at the Pass," one of them warned, "but follow our footprints and you can make it."

"If we hurry," Isobel added to herself. They dared not stop for a noon meal so she shared a piece of bread and cheese with Danny as they rode. The snow grew deeper and deeper, but the winding trail of footprints led them to the top at last.

Light snow was falling; it melted on Isobel's cheeks as she gazed out across the mountain ranges of Burma and China, remembering the magnificent sunset she had seen here. Today the view was hidden by lowering snow clouds that warned them to get across as quickly as they could. She shivered, wishing they had time to make a fire and heat some tea. But the wind rose, whirling snow into the tracks that marked the narrow path they must follow. To pause now would mean certain death.

Across the Pass and down the steep slope into Burma they went, slipping and sliding as the falling snow grew thicker. Jasper floundered into a drift up to his chest, so Isobel dismounted and Lucius hauled him back onto the trail. One of the men shifted Danny to carry him piggyback, which was easier and safer than the mountain chair. Danny, warm and dry in his raincoat and rubber hat, sat astride the broad Lisu shoulders and sang one song after another, cheering the whole party. Isobel wore a raincoat too, but the melting snow soaked her from the knees down and ran into her boots; soon her legs felt like blocks of ice.

On the lower slopes the snow turned to rain, and the steep path oozed with mud. Jasper began to lose his footing, so Isobel got off and trudged beside him on numb feet. It was an unspeakable relief to reach the village of Pien Ma four hours later, even though they received no welcome from the villagers.

Since it was still raining, they camped out in two ramshackle guest-house huts, where they made a smoky fire with green wood they had bought. Stiff and aching, Isobel shook out the quilts that she and Danny would sleep on. They were still streaked with damp from the trip down Pien Ma, but they would have to do. She spread them out on the bamboo floor, wrapped Danny in a blanket, and curled up beside him, trying to get warm.

At least we're out of Communist China, she told herself. Then her anxious thoughts ran on ahead. We still have ten days' trip through the jungle before we get to Myitkyina, and I have no visa—no permission even to be here in Burma. Abruptly she turned her mind to the rainstorm that beat against the flimsy walls of their shelter and dripped through the roof.

By now the snow at the top of the mountain would be deep. The Pass would surely be closed, probably for months. Even if she wanted to, there was no way she could go back. She smiled to herself in the smoky gloom. God had done it again. He'd arranged things so that all she could do was go forward—and trust in Him.

The next morning Isobel and her carriers began their long trek through the Burmese jungle. They saw signs of tigers and other wild animals, but they discouraged attacks by staying close together. Roads had been built years ago by the British, and after they passed the border district that had been razed by the Japanese, they found rest houses along the way. Isobel met a Burmese official who was a Christian, and he told her how to get a visa as soon as she reached Myitkyina. He also promised to radio Mr. Tegenfeldt, the American Baptist missionary in Myitkyina, to say that she was coming.

The first parting with her Lisu carriers came when they reached the motor road outside of Myitkyina. Now that she was safely through the mountains, the mountain-chair carriers needed to get back to their farms; they would take Jasper back with them too.

They started for China by a different route than they had come, and Isobel tried to smile as she waved good-bye. The rest of her carriers caught a truck into Myitkyina, excited about taking their first truck ride and seeing the big city. Now only Lucius waited with Danny and Isobel at the rest house beside the motor road.

The next morning, Mr. Tegenfeldt arrived in his jeep to pick them up, and he brought a delicious picnic lunch sent by his wife. The missionary was kind enough to suggest that they stay in his home, and Isobel accepted his offer gratefully.

As soon as they were on their way, Isobel asked, "Have you received a letter from the CIM about guaranteeing money for us?"

He frowned, then answered slowly, "No, I'm afraid we haven't."

What has happened to that letter? Isobel wondered, seriously alarmed. Has the Mission decided to cast me off because I left China? What am I going to do?

Exhausted from her long trip, she tried to give polite attention to what Mr. Tegenfeldt was saying. On the way into Myitkyina he pointed out Buddhist shrines, pagodas, and ruined temples; Kachin tribesmen, and plodding oxcarts. But Isobel felt like sitting down and crying. She and Danny still faced a journey halfway around the world, and how was she going to pay for it? She had only a few pieces of Chinese money and some blank checks from a bank in John's hometown in Pennsylvania. No one would believe that she had money in a bank so far away. *What am I going to do? What?* All the way into Myitkyina, the question seemed to grow larger and larger, swelling until she could think of nothing else.

When she reached the quietness of her bedroom in the Tegenfeldt's home, she knelt down and poured out her fears to the Lord. The only verse that came to mind was something Christ had said to his disciples: *Be not afraid.*

"Lord, please take this fear out of my heart," she said. "Yes. Thank you. And what should I do next?"

Well, of course she had to report her presence to the Burmese authorities. Then, she had to get some money. Quite a lot of money. The railroad had been bombed, so she and Danny would have to fly to Rangoon. From there they might be able to get passage to America on a ship.

What about Mr. Tegenfeldt? She was a stranger to him; would he trust her enough to cash a check? When she timidly raised the question, Mr. Tegenfeldt shook his head. No, he couldn't, he told her; then he suggested that she try one of the shops in the business district.

Be not afraid. Isobel clutched at her verse again, picked up her checkbook, and started off. She and Lucius decided that they would first try to find a store owned by someone who spoke English. As they walked down the street, a tall Hindu man greeted her, smiling. "Good morning," he said.

Isobel stepped into his shop, took a deep breath, and asked if he could cash a check for $150 on an American bank. To her surprise, he agreed. Later, when she happily showed Mr. Tegenfeldt her roll of Burmese money, she learned that Christian missionaries were so respected in Burma that any businessman would cash a check for them without hesitation. No wonder he hadn't seemed worried about it.

Arrangements were made quickly with Mr. Tegenfeldt's help, and soon Isobel and Danny were waiting at the airport to board their plane for Rangoon. Lucius stood quietly beside her, but from here she would go on alone. This was the moment she had dreaded ever since she had decided to leave China. She would never see Lucius again. How could she say good-bye to him, her faithful friend for so many years?

I will be strong; I won't make a scene, she told herself, and she smiled into his loving brown face, wrinkling now with dismay.

One last handshake; then, blinded by tears, she struggled up the steps into the noisy plane. She settled Danny as comfortably as she could on a hard, dirty seat and committed her aching heart once more to God.

Chapter Twenty-one

As the plane lumbered into the air and Isobel began to wonder what lay ahead, she remembered the note that one of the travelers arriving from Rangoon had passed on to her. It must be from someone in Rangoon, she thought as she unfolded the sheet of paper. Eric Cox! He was an old friend, and just seeing his name gave her courage. He had stopped at the guest house in Rangoon, heard that she and Danny were coming, and had found a place for them to stay. Since he was on his way to see his children in America, he suggested that perhaps they could take the same ship.

Danny bounced up and down in his seat when he heard they would be traveling with Uncle Eric, and Isobel could only praise the Lord for this new evidence of His loving-kindness.

At Rangoon, she discovered that no ships to America were available unless she wanted to wait six months. Meanwhile, Eric Cox had learned that if they flew to Hong Kong, they might be able to get on a freighter. He had to go on ahead but would send her word if they could travel on the same ship. Hong Kong it was, Isobel decided. Besides, a treasurer for the CIM was living in Hong Kong, and she could get the money she needed from him.

After Eric left, Isobel continued with the long process of getting approval from the immigration authorities and from the American consulate. Then Eric sent them a telegram from Hong Kong: BOAT LEAVING SATURDAY. ERIC.

Too bad, thought Isobel. We'll never make it to Hong Kong by Saturday. Since she was a Canadian, she had to get certain inoculations and have a physical examination before she was allowed to enter the States; it all took time. In fact, she couldn't help thinking, everything was taking an unreasonably long time. It had been late February when she left John at Olives; now it was early April, almost Easter.

When at last they were permitted to leave Rangoon, the only flight Isobel could get included a thirty-six–hour stopover in Bangkok, Thailand.

When they arrived in Bangkok, her first thought was, this is Saturday, the day Eric's ship leaves Hong Kong. I wish we were on it. And tomorrow is Easter Sunday. Her mind returned to the loved ones she had left behind. Homesickness swept through her as she remembered the Easter services they would be having tomorrow in Olives.

On Sunday morning she went down to the hotel lobby to see if she could find a church with services in English. But the desk clerk only looked at her blankly when she asked, and no matter what she tried, he seemed unable to give her any information. Finally she hired a pedicab on her own and found the American Bible Society, where she and Danny were kindly received by the missionaries there.

That afternoon, as she and Danny walked back through the richly furnished lobby of the hotel, the desk clerk summoned her to take a phone call. It was the Siamese Airlines office; they insisted that she get a visa for Danny before she could travel to Hong Kong.

This is ridiculous, Isobel thought. A six-year-old doesn't need a visa! And here I am, stranded at this expensive hotel—I'll have to pay another day's charges. That's ten dollars! I just don't have it. Anxiously she asked the desk clerk if they would accept a check on her American bank, and he raised a disdainful eyebrow. "We take only Siamese money or American cash, Madame. Not checks."

Back to her room she went. "Lord, I'm a stranger in this country," she prayed. "And now I need money again. What shall I do?" She sat down to read her Bible and found Isaiah 65:24. *Before they call, I will answer.*

"Yes, Lord, thank you," she whispered. "That's a nice verse. But what does it mean for us—now?" As she prayed, she remembered the inner compartment of her purse. At two different times in the past six months she had received gifts from America: a five-dollar bill and a ten-dollar bill. Since she had no use for American money, she had slid the bills into the zippered pocket of her purse.

"Oh, Lord, how wonderful You are," she cried. "You had the answer all ready."

On Monday they obtained Danny's visa, and on Tuesday they flew to Hong Kong. As they left the airplane, Danny cried, "Uncle Eric!" There stood Eric Cox, beaming at them. His ship had been delayed by leaking boilers, and there was just enough time for Isobel and Danny to get aboard. Uncle Eric's company made the long sea voyage a welcome adventure for Danny, and Isobel took the opportunity to rest.

Friends and family met them at Vancouver. Then they took a train across the continent to see Kathryn, who was now a college student in Illinois. There Isobel and Danny lived briefly with friends and later settled into a quiet apartment. Compared with her pioneer existence and the terrors of war, life in a small town with its peaceful, shaded streets seemed luxurious. She enjoyed making new friends and carrying out the simple routines of family life. Slowly her taut nerves began to relax, and her thoughts turned to the future.

John was still in China, but she knew that the CIM would never be allowed to operate under the Communist regime; he would come home eventually. Perhaps she and John and the children could live together as a family from now on. They had done pioneer missionary work for more than twenty years; it would be so good to rest for a while. And she already knew of an opportunity for Christian work here in America.

Just as Isobel had suspected, it wasn't long before John was forced out of the Salween Canyon at the point of a bayonet. But instead of being permitted to exit through Burma, he was required to journey all the way across China to Hong Kong. Meanwhile, the CIM was reorganizing into the Overseas Missionary Fellowship of the China Inland Mission. After eighty-five years in China, they would focus now on reaching unevangelized tribes and the Chinese people who lived in countries nearby.

Isobel's spirits sagged when she heard of the CIM's plans. She had a sudden vivid image of herself as a pioneer again: struggling up one rocky slope after another, living without electricity or running water. But she was almost fifty years old now, and tired. Immediately she wrote to John, "Please do not offer for the new fields until you get home and we can discuss everything together."

In July 1951, when John crossed over the Liberty Bridge at Hong Kong, he received her letter. Right away he telegraphed a reassuring answer. The Mission had asked him to spend a month or so surveying the tribes in North Thailand before he returned to the States. But he added, "I have not promised anything. . . . Truly no decision would work out satisfactorily if we were not united in heart about it."

Meanwhile, Isobel had been reading a book by Amy Carmichael, *Figures of the True*. One of its pictures reminded her of the snowy, windswept heights of Pien Ma Mountain. Beside the picture were a few paragraphs about mountaineering, and one terse sentence burned into her soul: *Climb or die.* That is so true for mountain climbing, she thought, remembering their desperate, nonstop journey over the Pass. And it's true for Christians—for me. If I falter now in my service for the Lord—if I look for the easy way out—I'll end up in spiritual decay.

She stared at the picture for a long time, and she was still thinking about it when John came home full of enthusiasm for the new doors that were opening. The government of Thailand was friendly, and the tribes in the north were willing to listen to the gospel. Many of the tribespeople understood Chinese, including more than 5,000 Lisu who had never heard the gospel. Yes, they would have to learn Thai, and it was mountainous country, but he and Isobel were experienced, and they could be a big encouragement to the younger missionaries.

Mountains to climb, thought Isobel. *Climb or die.* She knew then that the Lord had been preparing her for this new adventure.

* * * * *

The ruffled, muddy-brown surface of the Chao Prya River parted smoothly around the prow of their ship as Isobel studied the jungle that slipped past on either side. Thailand! This lonely, tangled expanse was so different from China's crowded riverbanks. Except for scattered clearings where bamboo huts perched on stilts, she had seen no sign of human life. They had shared the silent river with only a few barges and some teak logs floating downstream. Who lived here, besides snakes and scorpions and other jungle creatures?

After a while, she began to see fishermen and farmers, and women wearing brightly colored blouses and skirts. The boat turned into a smaller branch of the river and continued its leisurely journey. Fishing boats became more numerous, and a boy with his buffalo passed by. Late in the day, they dropped anchor in front of a town. These houses too stood on stilts, but they were made of teak wood. Above them towered palm trees, shadowy against the glowing colors of the sunset.

A richly ornamented building near the dock caught her eye. It was decorated with tiny, intricate sculptures, and the corners of its roof turned up into fanciful curves; joined to it was a taller building, tiered like a wedding cake and crowned with a slender spire. "What's that?" she asked John.

"It's a Buddhist wat," he said. "Like a temple, but they use it for a monastery and a school too. See the bells high up on the roof?" On the breeze came the soft tinkling of hundreds of tiny bronze bells.

Dusk began to fall as they stood there, and the Buddhist temple darkened into a silhouette that loomed black against the golden sky.

It had looked impressive in the daylight, Isobel thought, but now it seemed sinister and unyielding, a symbol of the dark religions that ruled in Thailand. So many religions—Buddhism, Islam, Confucianism. So many people! And among them were thousands of Lisu, hidden away in little mountain villages.

She gripped the ship's rail, her mind swinging across the miles to her Lisu children left behind in China. No, she mustn't grieve for them. They knew the true God, and He would care for them, just as He had cared for her all these years.

She took a last look at the hulking black outline of the temple, then she gazed past it to the dark horizon, to the unseen hills beyond. *Climb or die.* Nothing else mattered.

Epilogue: The Summit

1952-57

Epilogue

For the next two years, Isobel worked with John in North Thailand. She took on the heavy responsibility of hostess at the CIM base in Chiengmai, which served the needs of young missionaries studying Thai, departing tribal workers, and travel-worn missionaries.

During this time she also made trips into the mountains—exploratory trips with John, and settling-in trips with young missionary women who were going to live in a tribal village. On several occasions they visited Lisu villages, and although the Lisu dialect in Thailand was different, they could still preach the gospel. These Lisu did not seem to do much singing, but when Isobel introduced a few of the hymns she had translated, they responded with enthusiasm.

In 1954, however, Isobel discovered that she had cancer, and after surgery she returned to the United States for therapy. It was then that God launched her into a far-reaching ministry that He been been preparing her for during the last twenty years.

Isobel's reputation as an author was already well established. During her first furlough, she had written *Precious Things of the Lasting Hills,* which described her early experiences in Lisu country and introduced Homay and Joseph. On her second furlough she wrote *Nests Above the Abyss,* telling the story of several stalwart Lisu Christians, and *Second Mile People,* giving brief, loving profiles of men and women whom she held in high regard. *Stones of Fire,* written after she and Danny escaped from the Communists, told the story of Lucius and Mary, whose lives had been so closely intertwined with her own.

She had also written countless prayer letters, enthusiastic accounts of missionary work that sparkled with fascinating details. Over the years, her letters resulted in faithful prayer partners and a wide circle of friends who were deeply interested in the work of missions and wanted to know more about the Lisu tribe.

After several months of therapy in Philadelphia, Isobel felt much stronger. She and eleven-year-old Danny moved to Illinois where they shared an apartment, and while Danny went to school, she began to write the books that thousands of readers still cherish.

Ascent to the Tribes told about the Mission's further work in North Thailand, including her own involvement, and *Green Leaf in Drought Time* recounted the experiences of Dr. Rupert Clarke and Arthur Matthews, the last two CIM missionaries to escape from Communist China. Then came *By Searching* and *In the Arena,* telling the adventuresome story of her own life from a mature spiritual perspective.

Besides contributing to *Spiritual Food,* a magazine for tribal Christians who had refugeed into Burma, Isobel kept up a correspondence with her Lisu family. She was especially encouraged when Lucius wrote to say that the RSBS had eighty students and the Lisu evangelists were still ministering.

The writing schedule she had set for herself required stern discipline, but Isobel drew strength from a quiet confidence in God's enabling. Her trust in God, undaunted by pain and discomfort, was reflected by a remark she made in a letter to her brother, Murray.

I have proved God so often that I know He only chooses the best for me. . . . When He allows an evil, it is for the purpose of bringing greater blessing than if it had not happened. He makes Satan overstep himself and then takes spoils from him.

Meanwhile, Kathryn had graduated from college and was accepted as a missionary by the CIM. As her sailing date drew near, she and Isobel pondered the reality that Isobel could not live until Kathryn's first furlough. Should she stay and spend these last months or years with her mother?

It pierced the mother-side of me, Isobel wrote later, but they prayed about it and together agreed that Kathryn should not delay. She sailed for North Thailand in February 1955. Frequent letters flew back and forth between mother and daughter. When Kathryn wrote to tell of her engagement to Don Rulison, already a friend of the family, Isobel rejoiced at the good news.

She wasn't well enough to travel to the wedding in Chiengmai, North Thailand, but plenty of photographs were taken and rushed to her by air. She slipped them into the folder she had waiting, and they gave her great pleasure.

During her last months, Isobel found many joys. "The edelweiss of God," she called them, thinking of the bright-eyed, woolly plants that grow on rough mountain slopes. Loving friends; good books; letters, cards, flowers, and gifts—all these she counted as edelweiss.

That last New Year of 1957, the Lord gave her a verse from Isaiah 46, and she shared it with John, always at her bedside: *I am God, and there is none like me, Declaring the end from the beginning. . . . My counsel shall stand, and I will do all my pleasure.*

His pleasure, His will, had become her own; and she had proved the truth of Dante's words, *In His will is our peace.*

Still confident in God, still trusting, she rested her heart upon His will as she drew near to the summit; and there, on March 20, 1957, she met Him face to face.

Author's Note

After 1951, when all CIM missionaries were evacuated from China, reliable news about the Lisu church became scarce. We do know that over the years the Communists have made a determined effort to eliminate Christianity from China. One of their most effective tools has been the formation of all religious groups into one government-controlled church. Visitors to China observed that these churches, the only ones permitted to operate, were showcase churches, sparsely attended. Since meetings of more than three people had been declared illegal, many evangelical pastors and leaders were arrested, subjected to brainwashing by Communist experts, and then sent to labor camps for fifteen to twenty years.

By 1969, although the Cultural Revolution had lost its impetus, the Chinese Communists proclaimed that traditional Christianity was dead in China. But behind blanketed windows, attended only by family members, church services were being held in secret. The church was still alive. In following years, the underground church became bolder, reaching out to the young people who were disillusioned with the emptiness of Communist materialism. Large gatherings of believers sprang up in rural areas, and Bible studies were held openly.

Visitors are not allowed into the Salween Canyon, where the Kuhns worked, but Anthony Lambert of OMF International's Chinese Ministries has made several visits to Yunnan Province. He writes:

> Last September [1993] I was talking with the chief pastor in Kunming: he estimates there [are] about 200,000 Lisu Christians in China. From another source I was told there are over 1,300 churches among the Lisu. A recent Hong Kong Christian visitor was informed that local Chinese Communist officials were seriously considering whether the Lisu should be officially recognised as a "Christian tribe" — if so, they would be the only one so nominated in China! This figure of 200,000 compares with a total of 14,800 in 1950. . . . This is amazing testimony to the power of God's Word and the solid foundation provided by the Kuhns and others.

On the other hand, in the February/March 1994 issue of *China Insight,* Lambert reports the continuing concerns of Christian pastors in China. They warn that while Christians in some areas seem to have more freedom to evangelize, repression is far from over. As recently as January 1994, independent house churches in many parts of China were being restricted and harassed. Christian workers face tight surveillance, close monitoring of their personal lives, and constant pressure to cooperate with the government. Clearly, spiritual warfare still rages in China; but God is still sovereign, and He still answers prayer on behalf of Chinese and Lisu souls.

For Further Reading

Books about Isobel Kuhn's life:

By Searching by Isobel Kuhn; OMF Books. Mrs. Kuhn tells of her early experiences, from college years to the day she sailed for China.

In the Arena by Isobel Kuhn; OMF Books. A thoughtful look by Mrs. Kuhn at her years of missionary life in China.

Ascent to the Tribes by Isobel Kuhn; OMF Books. Mrs. Kuhn describes her pioneering experiences and the work of other missionaries in North Thailand.

Books about Lisu Christians:

Nests Above the Abyss by Isobel Kuhn; OMF Books. A glimpse into the lives of Lisu Christians in southwest China, with excerpts from Mrs. Kuhn's letters.

Stones of Fire by Isobel Kuhn; OMF Books. The true story of Mary, a young Lisu tribeswoman who lived near the Kuhns in southwest China.

Books about other people who were important to Isobel Kuhn:

Green Leaf in Drought Time by Isobel Kuhn; OMF Books. Mrs. Kuhn describes the escape of the last two CIM missionaries from Communist China.

Hudson Taylor, Vol. 1 by Dr. and Mrs. Howard Taylor; OMF Books. The story of Hudson Taylor's early life.

Hudson Taylor, Vol. 2 by Dr. and Mrs. Howard Taylor; OMF Books. The story of Hudson Taylor's later life and the growth of the China Inland Mission.

Mountain Rain by Eileen Crossman; OMF Books. The story of James O. Fraser's life, written by his daughter.

Second Mile People by Isobel Kuhn; OMF Books. The stories of six friends whose lives made a deep impression on Mrs. Kuhn.